Connecting with Kids through Stories

of related interest

First Steps in Parenting the Child Who Hurts
Tiddlers and Toddlers
Second Edition
Caroline Archer
ISBN 1 85302 801 0

Next Steps in Parenting the Child Who Hurts
Tykes and Teens
Caroline Archer
ISBN 1 85302 802 9

Trauma, Attachment and Family Permanence
Fear Can Stop You Loving
Edited by Caroline Archer and Alan Burnell for Family Futures
ISBN 1 84310 021 5

The Child's Own Story
Life Story Work with Traumatized Children
Richard Rose and Terry Philpot
ISBN 1 84310 287 0

The Adoption Experience
Families Who Give Children a Second Chance
Ann Morris
ISBN 1 85302 783 9

The Birth of an Adoptive, Foster or Stepmother
Beyond Biological Mothering Attachments
Barbara Waterman
ISBN 1 84310 724 4

Helping Children to Build Self-Esteem
A Photocopiable Activities Book
Deborah Plummer
ISBN 1 85302 927 0

Connecting with Kids through Stories

Using Narratives to Facilitate Attachment in Adopted Children

*Denise B. Lacher, Todd Nichols
and Joanne C. May*

Jessica Kingsley Publishers
London and Philadelphia

First published in 2005
by Jessica Kingsley Publishers
116 Pentonville Road
London N1 9JB, UK
and
400 Market Street, Suite 400
Philadelphia, PA 19106, USA

www.jkp.com

Copyright © Attachment and Family Center of Minnesota 2005

Library of Congress Cataloging in Publication Data
A CIP catalog record for this book is available from the Library of Congress

British Library Cataloguing in Publication Data
A CIP catalogue record for this book is available from the British Library

ISBN-13: 978 1 84310 797 2
ISBN-10: 1 84310 797 X

Printed and Bound in Great Britain by
Athenaeum Press, Gateshead, Tyne and Wear

Contents

Acknowledgments

Our colleagues at the Family Attachment and Counseling Center contributed valuable and honest feedback, nurturing, and lots of chocolate. We would like to thank Melissa Nichols, an excellent writer herself, who gave us direction in times when we could not find the words. Jan Norman, Maren Harris, and Heather Cargill contributed their wisdom and frequently reminded us that, yes, we could do this. Our readers also gave us much-needed comments and suggestions: Marti Erickson, Greg Keck, Dan Hughes, Ginny Blade, Marcia Mans, Jack Wallinga, and Connie Dummer.

Most of all we would like to thank the parents and children who have shared their experiences of hurt, pain, and anger as well as success and joy with us. Our lives have been blessed and changed by them. Each and every narrative inspired and challenged the methodology, taking it places we had not yet imagined. We really could not have done this without them.

Denise

Thank you, Scott, for listening, encouraging, and shouldering more than your share when there were not enough hours in the day. Holly and Annie, sharing your journey through life has taught me so much about attachment, child development, and parenting. Thanks for not giving up on this "less than perfect" mom; I'm still learning. Mom and Dad, I'm really glad that I can say, "I'm getting more and more like you the older I get." And Todd, it's been a longer road than we thought, but made much easier by your friendship.

Todd

Melissa, Jeremy, Anna, and Grace – what a wonderful family with which I've been blessed! You continue to add so much to my life. Thank you all for your constant support and teaching. Mom, the older I get, the more I appreciate your wisdom. Thank you, Denise, for your tireless writing and rewriting. You're a wonderful person to work with.

Joanne

I would like to thank the hundreds of parents who contributed to the development of Family Attachment Narrative Therapy and the writing of this book.

Legacy of an Adopted Child

Once there were two women, who never knew each other.
One you do not remember, the other you call Mother.
Two different lives shaped to make you one.
One became your guiding star, the other became your sun.
The first one gave you life. The second one taught you to live it.
The first gave you a need for love, the second was there to give it.
One gave you a nationality, the other gave you a name.
One gave you a talent, the other gave you aim.
One gave you emotions, the other calmed your fears.
One saw your first sweet smile, the other dried your tears.
One sought for you a home she could not provide.
The other prayed for a child and her hope was not denied.
And now you ask me through your tears,
The age-old question unanswered through the years.
Heredity or environment, which are you a product of?
Neither my darling, neither,
Just two different kinds of love.

Author unknown

Introduction

Just two different kinds of love.

On a warm spring morning Todd and his wife, Melissa, were walking through a park to meet a colleague for breakfast. She is a child psychiatrist who has worked in the field of attachment and bonding for many years. Over granola and a large latte, she asked about our work with maltreated children. After a brief explanation of what we do, she leaned forward and asked incredulously, "So parents tell them stories and they get better?" Again and again, professionals and parents ask us some version of this question. Yes, it sounds too easy, too good to be true. But stories indeed make a difference.

At the Family Attachment and Counseling Center, we specialize in working with children who have trouble connecting with their parents, families, and peers. These children typically have suffered from early care that was insensitive and inconsistent at best, neglectful and abusive at worst. When early life relationships do not provide the kind of emotional and physical care that is required for optimal growth and development, children may face difficulties in how they see themselves, others, and the world. This basic sense of security or insecurity forms a model or pattern for relationships with people. This *inner working model* affects a child's thoughts, feelings, and behavior.

Parenting children with an insecure attachment and a negative, mistaken model for relationships is extremely challenging. Loving them is not always enough. Likewise, thousands of attuned, caring responses may not be sufficient to repair the damage done by traumatic early experiences. The most talented, insightful, and experienced parent may want at times to give in to total despair, thinking that they can never reach their child. When parents live with a challenging child, every day provides a never-ending supply of "incidents" that motivate their search for help. We are not exaggerating when we say that most parents we encounter have read more books on parenting than we have. They look to professionals – teachers, social workers, therapists, and psychiatrists – for help. Their desire to help a hurt and hurting child is strong.

In 1995, we began using stories as our primary therapeutic modality in reaching these troubled children. In our attachment program, parents construct and tell stories to their children to chip away at mistaken beliefs that were formed by their past experiences. We called this new treatment Family Attachment Narrative Therapy. This book is a natural outgrowth of the belief that parents are the best hope to heal a child who has been hurt in life. Each parent has an innate ability to assess his or her child's needs and meet them. Family Attachment Narrative Therapy is easy to learn. It is a natural and enjoyable way to help and teach children. *Claiming, trauma, developmental,* and *successful child* narratives are tailored to the child's individual situation and grounded in a parent's understanding of the child's individual characteristics and nuances. Family Attachment Narrative Therapy can provide a vehicle to address problematic behavior in a way that increases the connection, or attachment, between the parent and child. Parents who have used Family Attachment Narrative Therapy have found that it helps them connect with their child, helps the child heal from his past, and teaches him new ways of behaving at home, in the school, and in the community.

Although the book is written in a "how to" format, it is not designed to present a "one size fits all" answer to parenting. We have found that the meaning of the behavior is unique to each child, and proper and effective solutions require piecing together this meaning. This is the work of the parent – someone who knows and desires a lasting relationship with a child. *Connecting with Kids through Stories* looks at the possible causes of difficult behavior and provides a way to understand and work with a child who is troubled. Chapter 1 describes the formation of the child's inner working model in response to attachment experiences, life events, and level of development. How to discover the child's unique model and piece together the meaning of behavior is the focus of Chapter 2. Chapter 3 describes parental attunement and outlines how to tell the narratives that bond, heal, and teach. Chapters 4, 5, 6, and 7 explain each category of parent narrative: *claiming, trauma, developmental,* and *successful child.* The examples given throughout the book are just that – examples, designed to help readers understand how to construct narratives for children. The best stories for each child will be different from the examples. Attuned parents who understand the meaning of their child's behavior will be able to develop unique and fun stories that help and teach their child.

We've made extensive use of examples which we hope will illustrate the variety and richness of the approach. The story of fictional parents (Bill and Karen) and their adopted child (Robert) is developed throughout the book and placed at opportune locations in the text to illustrate the methodology. Readers explore the impact of maltreatment on Robert's development, born to a 15-year-old chemically dependent mother, and the formation of his inner working model. The story continues as Karen and Bill, frustrated by Robert's behaviors, work with a therapist to piece together the complex inner working model behind Robert's behavior and develop narratives to help him heal. Additional vignettes of other children are used to illustrate the technique, and are sprinkled throughout the text, often on tinted panels. Many of the examples are based on real clients, but in all cases identifying information has been altered to protect confidentiality. Actual examples of stories are placed throughout Chapters 4 to 7.

Connecting with Kids through Stories is intended to help families struggling with very difficult and complex issues. Insecure attachment, traumatic life experiences, and developmental issues may cause behavior problems in children that challenge even the most experienced parents. Our hope is that Family Attachment Narrative Therapy will be a powerful tool. When used to address the issues underlying the behavior, the child's negative inner working model is transformed. A new, healthy model changes the child's view of himself, of the adults around him, and of the world. Stories do have the power to change a life.

Note

In light of the controversy surrounding attachment therapy, we feel that it is important to draw a distinction between Family Attachment Narrative Therapy and some other approaches. Attachment therapy is often considered to be coercive holding therapy or some form of therapy which uses controlling, confrontational techniques. Family Attachment Narrative Therapy is a gentle, nonprovocative, nonintrusive methodology in which parents are the primary agents of healing their hurt child.

Chapter 1

The Inner Working Model

Two different lives shaped to make you one.
One became your guiding star, the other became your sun.

Robert was not a wanted child. Tanya was 15. She didn't want to be a mother. She smoked, sometimes a pack a day. She liked to hang out and party with her friends. Someone always managed to get some weed and a bottle. When the nurse at the clinic asked about drug and alcohol use she always denied it. She didn't want trouble and what difference would it make anyway? Tanya had been placed in a group home with other teenagers after running away from home. She said her mother's boyfriend hit her and she couldn't stay there one more minute. She would be moving back home after the baby was born. Her mother promised that the boyfriend would be gone by then.

When the baby was born, Tanya was terrified. The pain was bad. She didn't want to hold him after she gave birth; she just wanted to curl up and sleep. She watched the nurses fuss and coo at him. "Let them," she thought. When she arrived home with Robert, the boyfriend was there, drunk and mean as ever. He yelled every time the baby cried. Tanya's mom told her to feed him; she tried but he just kept crying. So she left and found her friends. When she got back, Robert was sleeping on her bed. She slept too.

Robert felt uncomfortable, hungry, wet, and alone most of the time. He cried a lot. Sometimes someone came and other times he fell asleep exhausted. Sometimes someone came and his head exploded in hurt and he cried harder. As the weeks passed, he stopped crying much. His bottom was raw and sore but he didn't cry. When he was fed he ate as fast as he could. There were lots of people, lots of noise, and nothing made sense. He rubbed his cheek on the mattress and held his bottle tight. When he learned to crawl, and then walk, he discovered that he could get what he wanted all by himself. He learned that sometimes when he toddled up to the big people, they smiled, offered treats and played with him. At other times when he would do the same thing, he would be pushed or shoved away. He couldn't figure out what he had done wrong. He still tried to get what he wanted; he was just more careful. The big people left him alone most of the time. Sometimes they yelled at him and said he was bad, ugly, and stupid. He didn't know what that meant but it hurt; kind of like the other hurt but this hurt didn't go away. Sometimes they played with him but he never let his guard down. He expected more hurt.

...and so it begins...the formation of the inner working model

The meaning a child makes of his early life experiences and the behaviors he develops in response to those experiences have an impact not only on the child's future but the future of the child's family, neighbors, and community. A child draws conclusions about himself and his world in relation to early life experiences. A child is more likely to draw positive conclusions in response to early relationships characterized by nurturing and consistency. In the case of a child with negative early life experiences, such as Robert, the child is at higher risk of developing negative conclusions. A child in this situation is more likely to manifest behaviors that make him more of a challenge to parent. In many cases, the child is finally removed from his birth family. Nonetheless, the conclusions formed in early life may stick with him and inhibit his ability to lead a productive, cooperative, connected life with others, particularly his new caretakers. Some children may possess the resiliency to overcome a beginning such as Robert's. But for many other children these experiences will engender social, emotional, and behavioral problems throughout their life span.

The power of a parent's smile, touch, and loving interactions is enormous. Unfortunately, traumatic early life experiences are far too common in our society. Prenatal exposure to alcohol and drugs, abuse and neglect, influences the child's development. The child's experience of attachment relationships, life events, course of development, and core beliefs are collectively referred to in this book as the *inner working model*. Understanding the inner working model is the key to doing Family Attachment Narrative Therapy. The inner working model develops in early childhood. Like snowflakes, no two are alike. And, like snowflakes, the complexity and beauty can only be seen if closely examined one at a time. The model is unique to the individual. Figure 1.1 depicts the formation of the inner working model. The three spheres – attachment and relationship experiences, life events and trauma, and development – are interconnected, and each influences the meaning the child draws from those early experiences. Each sphere – attachment, life events, and development – is discussed separately below.

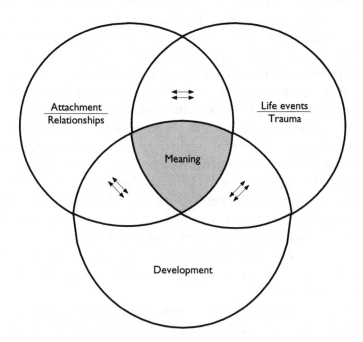

Figure 1.1: The inner working model. Loving or terrifying attachment experiences influence numerous aspects of development. Life events influence brain development and the child's ability to relate to others. A child's growth and development along an adaptive, normal pathway can be altered by early experiences such as abuse or neglect.

Attachment relationships

Attachment is about connections between people. John Bowlby (1969/1982, 1973, 1980) introduced *attachment theory* to describe behaviors he had observed between parents and children. In infants, these behaviors are designed to maintain closeness with an attachment figure that provides support and security. The level of attachment security depends partly on whether the parent is emotionally and physically available and responsive to the infant's needs. When an infant is under stress he makes noises, cries, and moves to get the attention of the caregiver. Those attachment behaviors stop when the primary caretaker soothes, comforts, and relieves the stress. Although most evident in infancy and early childhood, attachment behaviors – ways of moving closer and connecting with the parent and other significant people in life – are present in adolescence and adulthood. As the child grows, the attachment figure is utilized as a secure base from which the child moves out to explore and socialize (Ainsworth 1967). When the caretaker is nearby and watching he has the confidence to move away, pick up an interesting toy, or join another child in the sandbox. By one year of age children develop patterns of attachment behaviors in response to the quality of the relationship with their primary caregiver. These patterns are an enduring set of specific behaviors that infants, toddlers, and children use when interacting with parents, caregivers, and other adults. Identifying the child's dominant attachment pattern is useful in discovering his inner working model. It provides clues to what might have happened back then, what he missed out on, and what he might need from current caregivers.

Attachment behavior patterns may be organized or disorganized. When a child displays purposeful behavior designed to elicit a response from the parent, his attachment style is classified as organized. Smiling and approaching the parent with outstretched arms is an example of organized behavior. So is screaming, throwing toys, and moving away from a parent who is entering the room. Organized patterns include three types: secure, anxious resistant (ambivalent), and anxious avoidant (Ainsworth *et al.* 1978).

Secure attachments flourish when the caregiver is attuned and responsive to the child. Attunement (Siegel 1999, 2001) is a highly sensitive state in which parents are able to respond to the individual needs of the child. A sensitive parent recognizes the child's physical and mental state, whether the child is bored, lonely, uncomfortable, content, etc. A sensitive parent responds to the child's needs by providing comfort, nurturing, or stimulation. The child then perceives the caregiver as loving and available when he is stressed. A securely attached infant clearly recognizes and prefers the attachment figure. He may even calm down when the parent enters the room anticipating that his need will be satisfied. A securely attached toddler will confidently explore the environment under the parent's watchful eye. He frequently checks in with the parent by seeking eye contact or a quick hug, showing her his toy or presenting her with the picture he has just created. Securely attached children may protest when the parent leaves; however, they are able to tolerate increasingly longer periods of separation without being overwhelmed with feelings of distress. They look forward to the parents' return and happily greet them, initiating physical contact.

When the parent lacks such attunement and responsiveness and is inconsistent in responding to the child's attachment behaviors, an ambivalent or resistant style of attachment may develop. In this relationship the parent's own needs and feelings seem to impair her ability to tune into what her child needs. Excitedly bouncing a tired, sleepy baby and angrily feeding a fussy but full baby are examples of a mismatch between the parent and child's states. Because the child is unsure that his needs will be satisfied, he may be preoccupied with any discomfort he experiences and dissatisfied with the parent's attempts to attend to him. In this behavior pattern the child may cling, resist separations, and be angry and difficult to soothe. We witnessed this style of attachment working with Frank and his new foster family.

> Frank was raised in a crack house where life was uncertain and chaotic. Now anything and everything could make him angry. He clutched his foster mother's leg with every ounce of strength he had while screaming, "Get away from me! Leave me alone! I hate you!" He hit when he was mad and then immediately kissed the spot, saying, "Are you OK?" The situation seems laughable, but parents living with a child who has an ambivalent attachment feel drained and exhausted by the never-ending demands for attention and the constant anger and attacks. A child who is ambivalently attached focuses all of his attention and energy on the parent or substitute caregiver, never trusting they will be available every time he has needs. "I can't trust you!" seems to be one of his underlying beliefs.

When a parent is insensitive to the child's state or ineffective at meeting his needs, the child becomes frustrated. A child who experiences such neglect may develop an anxious avoidant attachment pattern. An avoidantly attached child did not experience his parent as available. His signals for attention, nurturing, and comfort were largely ignored. The parent may have even rejected or punished him for being distressed. The child with an avoidant pattern of attachment does not expect the parent to be responsive. He avoids the frustration of those interactions by withdrawing or actively ignoring the parent. Outwardly he appears independent and self-sufficient.

> Ellen was a child with an avoidant style of relating to her parents. She had been placed with them for three years and her parents felt stuck. They felt no closer emotionally to her than the day she came. She wasn't aggressive or destroying property like some of their friends' adopted children so they felt lucky in some ways. Sometimes they wondered if they even needed help; maybe they were expecting too much. Ellen simply wouldn't allow them to be her parents. Largely ignored unless she needed something, they felt used and manipulated. They were certain that as soon as Ellen turned 18 she would take off and never look back. "I don't need anyone!" seemed to be her motto.

Some children do not fit into one of the attachment categories that feature a somewhat organized way of interacting with the caregiver. Main and Solomon (1986, 1990) labeled the absence of a planned strategy in approaching the attachment figure as disorganized or disoriented. Disorganized attachment is often found in children who have been maltreated. The child is confused, trapped in the dilemma that the source of stress is the person from whom he is driven to seek comfort. Disorganized attachment may also be evident in families where there is no abuse taking place. Instead, parents may have unresolved trauma or loss in their own past. As a result, they experience rapid changes in mood and behavior or the child's behavior and needs trigger memories related to experiences in their family of origin. The parent's moods and resulting actions are unrelated to the child's signals and frighten the child. The child fears the parent yet has no other alternative if he is hungry or hurt. When a child is displaying disorganized attachment during a separation and reunion with his parent, his behavior seems to make no sense. He may display a mixture of approach and avoidance behaviors when in the presence of the caregiver. He may freeze as if in a trance, fall down, walk in circles, or walk toward the parent while looking in the opposite direction (Main and Solomon 1986, 1990). These children may eventually discover a way of dealing with their parent as they near school age (Main and Cassidy 1988). The child learns to manage the anxiety of interactions by controlling the parent.

Evan was bossy and mouthy to his mother. In response she threatened punishment but seldom followed through. He ignored the threats and his mother until eventually she gave in to keep the peace. If that didn't work, he blew up. By the time he had calmed down, neither of them could remember what he had been asked to do.

Heather was scared of her mother's anger and threats but could still control what she did by carefully manipulating her with kindness. Attuned to every nuance of her mother's moods, she stayed close by to comfort, soothe, and calm her. She danced silly dances to make her laugh, made her a cup of tea when she looked tired, and reminded her to take her medicine when she had a hard time getting out of bed in the morning.

Both Evan and Heather had finally found a way to stay close to their mothers, stay safe, and get what they wanted.

A strong secure attachment promotes the child's social and emotional development. A child's expectations of how the parent will respond tend to become enduring beliefs that he applies to other relationships (Main, Kaplan, and Cassidy 1985). Several studies suggest that attachment patterns in infancy may be related to the older child's behavior in relationships with others. Securely attached children who expect parents and others to respond positively to them are typically regarded as sociable, empathetic, compliant, less dependent, and as having better self-control. Insecurely attached children display maladaptive behaviors with others. (For the purposes of this book, an insecure attachment refers to the attachment classifications of ambivalent, avoidant, and disorganized.) A child with an anxious avoidant pattern of attachment is often described as angry, hostile, and withdrawn. He may lack the basic social skills necessary to find acceptance by his peers. Impulsive and demanding or withdrawn and fearful patterns of behavior were observed in anxious resistant children who are uncertain what kind of response, if any, they may get from a parent or peer. Observations of ambivalently attached children also revealed a lack of confidence in how to approach their environment. The disorganized child seems to alternate between aggressively defending himself from peers to withdrawing from any social situations that may be stressful. Anxiety and lack of experience result in responses that appear odd and weird to their peers. Screaming and dashing in to grab a toy or lying down in the middle of a group of children playing house are examples of the disorganized child's behavior in peer groups (Belsky and Cassidy 1994; Bretherton 1985; Elicker, Egeland, and Sroufe 1992; Erickson, Sroufe, and Egeland 1985).

Children with insecure patterns of relating express these negative expectations in their day-to-day behavior with parents, teachers, coaches, neighbors, and peers. Unfortunately an inaccurate model may hinder attachment to a new foster or adoptive parent after the child has been placed in another home. The child still expects parents to ignore, frustrate, or hurt him. Undeserving parents find themselves the target of behaviors that range from annoying chatter to aggressive assaults. A child with an insecure attachment develops defenses to protect himself

Tanya's relationship with her mother had always been a stormy one. Her mother's love and attention had been sporadic. When a boyfriend moved in and the parties began, it meant trouble. There would be fights, yelling, and hitting. She hated the times when her mom didn't get up in the morning. She would wake up to get ready for school but she never knew if she was early or late. There were never clean clothes and she knew the kids and teachers would whisper. She was scared to walk the six blocks alone. Things were better when there was no boyfriend around. Sometimes Tanya and her mom played or went to the park. When Tanya got older she yelled and fought back. She ran away from the chaos. She hung out with friends and stopped going to school. Tanya's experiences made it hard for her to feel anything toward her son. Immature and focused on her own needs, she was unable to read his cues. She responded in a random way to his cries or failed to respond at all. Hungry, uncomfortable, frightened, and mad, his heart raced. He startled easily. Every sensation increased his distress. His eyes, arms, and legs moved and he fussed constantly. Some infants give up at this point; not Robert. But the continuous stress changed the way his brain developed. The world didn't make sense to Robert. He was never sure what would happen. His home seemed dangerous and unpredictable. He learned to avoid contact with anything or anyone.

from a world he believes is unsafe and unpredictable. Although necessary, those same defenses make changing inaccurate models more difficult. Information that contradicts his current inner working model is screened from conscious thought. It seems as if he only notices and remembers negative events and dismisses anything positive that happens to him. A defended child's memory of the magic of Disney World may be "You didn't buy me anything." A perfect day at the lake is reduced to "I never get to drive the boat!" Although formation begins at an early age the models are not fixed. Models can be updated. As the child's capacity for memory and thinking develops, he is able to reassess experiences (Carlson and Sroufe 1995). Changes in the interactions and communications between parent and child can shift working models (Bowlby 1988; Bretherton 1987; Bretherton and Munholland 1999). That is what Family Attachment Narrative Therapy is all about. Time after time, we have seen narratives change beliefs, change behaviors, and change families.

Life events

Life is full of stress. Even positive and pleasant experiences cause stress. Children are better able to handle stress and strong emotions if they have developed a relationship with someone they can count on when they need help. The working model of a securely attached child anticipates comfort and reassurance from the attachment figure. This model may serve to protect the child from developing posttraumatic stress in response to experiences the child perceives as terrifying (Liotti 1999; van der Kolk and Fisler 1994). The working model of an insecurely attached child, however, may create a vulnerability to stress.

Beginning with Bowlby, theorists and researchers have hypothesized that attachment is more than an emotional bond of trust (Schore 2001a; Sroufe 1996). Attachment can also be viewed as a regulatory system vital to the infant's social-emotional development. Secure attachment relationships help children develop the capacity to regulate or manage emotional responses to everyday life experiences. An attachment relationship that provides security and safety seems to protect children from the effects of stress, even severe stress or traumatic life events. In contrast, early trauma, especially trauma that occurs within the parent–child relationship, may put the child at risk for developing psychological problems (Schore 2001b; Siegel 1999). Advances in brain-imaging technology have led to an explosion of research on the role of traumatic experiences on the developing brain (Perry 1997; Perry *et al.* 1995; Schore 1994; Siegel 1999). From the moment of conception, the brain is under constant change in response to life events. Secure attachment relationships nourish the brain. Trauma that takes place in those important relationships may be toxic to the developing brain of a child (Perry 1997; Siegel 1999, 2001).

The capacity for regulation is believed to be a function of the right hemisphere of the brain, the development of which dominates the child's first three years of life (Schore 2001a). In those first years, the mother or another primary caregiver is responsible for the external regulation of the child's level of arousal and emotional states. When the child is uncomfortable, upset, angry, or afraid, soothing actions by the parent help him return to a calm and quiet state. Internally, the mechanisms for self-regulation are forming. Attuned, sensitive responses to the child's cues help the child learn to regulate his emotions under stress. Trauma alters right brain development and impedes the child's ability to regulate strong feelings such as anger, fear, excitement, shame, hopelessness, and despair (Schore 2001b). At the same time relational trauma contributes to the development of negative inner working models, fosters negative feelings of self-worth, and impairs basic trust (van der Kolk 1996). Children who have experienced trauma are at risk for developing hostile, aggressive behavior in childhood and adolescence (Lyons-Ruth and Jacobvitz 1999). Trauma and related disruptions in attachment relationships have also been linked with emotional inflexibility and impairments in attention, interpersonal relationships, empathy, and coping capacity (Erickson *et al.* 1985).

Each child's stress reaction will be different. Some children withdraw physically in response to a perceived threat (flight). Other children may remain physically present but withdraw emotionally (another form of flight), thus avoiding psychological contact with what is stressful to them. Still others react aggressively as their stress level begins to rise. They may verbally or physically fight back. Hyperarousal (fight) and dissociation (flight) are normal responses that enable children to survive a neglectful and abusive environment (Perry *et al.* 1995). When the experiences of a child are overwhelmingly stressful, the brain tends to function in a continuous survival mode. In that mode the brain responds in a primitive, reactive way to stress. The child's ability to think and plan is impaired. Instead, emotions and impulses drive the child's behavior. Ever watchful and wary of danger, the child is constantly on the verge of a state of fight or flight. These strategies may well serve the child while enmeshed in the trauma, but problems occur when the child is removed from the dangerous environment and placed in a new home. For a parent this means that minor matters can cause major reactions. Asking a child to empty the dishwasher may not seem like a life-threatening situation to an adoptive or foster parent, but to a child sensitized to stress, it could cause a flight/fight response. Remember, even pleasant experiences cause some stress. Peering through the glass at zoo animals, being jostled in line for ice cream, and riding the zoo train all cause stress and could lead to a meltdown or a shutdown. Despite the new parents' efforts to love, comfort, nurture, and keep the child safe, the child's learned responses to stress can frustrate all attempts.

Contributing to the negative impact of trauma on the developing child is the child's inability to attribute the responsibility for the maltreatment appropriately. Only humans have the ability to judge and even personalize the traumatic experience and under stress children may fail to correctly assess the event (van der Kolk 1996). Children are great observers of the world around them but they are lousy interpreters (Dreikurs with Soltz 1990). Mistaken beliefs result in misguided decisions and actions. In addition, young children believe they are the center of the universe. If they have not progressed through this stage, they may fail to see the role others play in the traumatic life events. The meaning children assign to their early experiences is critical to their ability to resolve traumatic experiences. We have worked with siblings who went through the same trauma, yet formed different conclusions about the events. The younger sibling was in an earlier stage of development and attributed responsibility for the neglect and eventual abandonment at an orphanage to himself. He believed that if he had behaved better, he would not have been rejected by his birth family. His inner working model reflected those beliefs. He expected to be rejected by his adoptive parents. His feelings of shame and worry that his "badness" would be discovered contributed to the development of depression and anxiety. In contrast, the older sibling concluded that her birth parents' alcoholism was not her fault. She was old enough to recognize that alcoholism, drug use, and poverty were pervasive in her country. While sad and angry that her family could not overcome their difficulties and keep the family intact, she did not take responsibility for the disruption.

The meaning a child makes of his early experiences contributes to the developing inner working model. Clients with posttraumatic stress and the professionals who work with them know the effects of trauma are difficult but not impossible to treat. Beliefs and behaviors can change.

Research is now suggesting that the brain remains open to change throughout life. Reading a book, learning to dance, and conversing with an old friend all provide experiences that cause subtle changes in the brain. New experiences in a child's life may influence attachment patterns of behavior and the brain's regulatory systems (Siegel 2001). Family Attachment Narrative Therapy is a way parents can provide their children with new experiences, reshaping their working model and eventually their behavior.

> Robert experienced ongoing abuse and neglect that injured his developing brain. He was left alone for long periods of time without caring human interactions and sensory stimulation. Without loving touch, the sight of his mother's face, interesting toys to look at, sounds that aroused his curiosity, essential neurological connections were not made. Unable to regulate his responses to stress, he seemed inconsolable and Tanya often gave up trying to soothe him. Robert was easily overwhelmed when his senses were stimulated. Loud unexplained sounds caused terror. Touch that should have been pleasant was uncomfortable. Robert learned that some stress could be avoided if he just ignored what was happening around him. He didn't look at anyone or anything. Rubbing his cheek against the mattress, his eyes stared unfocused at the wall. Getting what he wanted also relieved the stress he felt. He became obsessed with getting what he wanted. Limits and restrictions by the adults around him intensified the emotions he was experiencing. Eventually a "no" triggered a full "flight/fight" response. Robert alternated between striking out aggressively and retreating to the safety of his mattress.

Development

Healthy growth and development depends on feeling safe and secure in the environment. If the child feels that his world is a dangerous place, then curiosity, exploration, and learning take a back seat to surviving.

The establishment of secure attachments in infancy is a principal developmental task. Successful completion of this first important task facilitates mastery of developmental tasks in later stages. Securely attached children develop skills that prepare them for increasingly independent functioning as they grow up (Erickson *et al.* 1985). Conversely, lack of a secure attachment increases the probability of a qualitative change in the normal developmental pathway. The child may follow a deviant pathway leading to antisocial and delinquent behavior (Egeland *et al.* 2002). In addition, other changes in development may occur due to prenatal exposure to chemicals, malnutrition, or other medical conditions such as chromosomal abnormalities and structural abnormalities of the central nervous system. The result is children who act much younger than their actual age.

As early as the nineteenth century Janet (1889, cited in Schore 2001b) observed that trauma impaired an individual's ability to "assimilate new experiences…as if their personality development has stopped at a certain point" (p.210). As discussed earlier, trauma results in a dysregulated emotional state in the infant or child. In this constant state of anxiety, the child focuses his energy on relieving the discomfort of stress. Some constantly seek the attention of caregivers at the expense of exploration, play, and social behaviors (Bowlby 1969/1982). Others shut down, escaping the source of stress. In both cases, the child's resources are focused on avoiding stress rather than mastering important developmental tasks. Stress and anxiety require enormous amounts of energy that are then unavailable for growth and learning. It is common to see that children raised in orphanages seem to blossom once adopted. In a safe environment, their development leaps ahead. Unfortunately, they may be months and years behind their peers and the catch-up process is usually not a smooth, steady progression. Learning a new language may take a few months; learning how to be part of a family is much more difficult.

Mark and his mother had lived with relatives or on the streets of a village in India most of his life. It was a dangerous and unpredictable life. She found a job in a city but could not work and care for him. He was left at the door of an orphanage at age three and never saw his mother again. His new parents adopted him when he was seven. But when compared with their toddler, he seemed to act more like a four-year-old than a first grader even after a year of consistent attention and love.

The parents we work with often observe that the child's development seems to have changed or slowed down at the point in his life where he lost his safety and security. Mark's parents believe he was stuck at a three-year-old level when they adopted him. Now they wonder if he will always be four years behind.

Maltreated children may have difficulty with common cognitive concepts such as object permanence, causality, and symbolic function. They struggle with feelings of anxiety when parents leave for work, when a teacher takes maternity leave, when their toys and belongings are out of sight. In the world that they came from, nothing was constant. And now, "out of sight" truly means "out of mind." Such a child resists separations from those closest to him and from beloved possessions. In addition, many children do not appear to have mastered cause and effect thinking. They repeat the same mistakes over and over, seldom learning from the consequences of their actions. Even after suffering injuries one child persisted in climbing to the top of furniture and jumping. Altered development is also revealed in a child's play. We have seen children who do not know how to play at a developmentally appropriate level. Toys are touched, dumped, lined up, and then put away without any actual play taking place. Imagination and pretend play are conspicuously absent. Most troubling to adoptive and foster parents is the apparent lack of conscience in children. Parents commonly report that their child shows no remorse or guilt. He laughs when others are hurt or angry. Unable to understand how someone else might feel, he seems puzzled and frustrated when he is given consequences. Also, as stated earlier, a child's emotional functioning may be impaired – he may become easily overwhelmed with strong feelings. Parents cannot reason with him. His behavior may have little organization and seems to be an unintentional reaction to feelings of anxiety or anger. Although children who suffered trauma in their early relationships struggle to master necessary tasks and stages, physical deficits, emotional and social delays, and negative beliefs hinder their progress.

Robert didn't play with toys the way other children did. He wandered around the house and neighborhood, watching, always watching. He would sometimes stand in front of the TV watching the constantly changing images. He seldom spoke. Robert had lots of feelings, but no way to name what he was feeling or express it. He was focused on getting and doing what he wanted even if it resulted in getting yelled at or hurt. Deprived of normal interactions with a caregiver, Robert's development detoured in a dangerous direction. He could not sit still, constantly misbehaved, and then fell apart when he was upset. To an outsider he may appear like a "spoiled brat"; however, his early experiences and lack of nurturing care have impeded his development of self-regulation, speech, attention, and conscience.

Meanings (or "peanut butter and a crib")

As shown in Figure 1.1, attachment, life events, and development are interconnected. Stress affects the nature and quality of attachment; attachment affects how events are perceived; and both, in turn, affect development. The shaded middle area is the meaning a person draws from the three spheres. It is the meaning that drives the child's behavior. If the meaning is shifted, healing takes place in all three spheres. If the meaning is not revised it may become entrenched, expanding as the person grows older. At some point the meaning gets so enlarged that the individual may no longer see the underlying influences. He believes that he is bad or worthless but can no longer see that these beliefs may be related to early attachment or trauma. The meaning becomes who he is. This model has applications for many psychological disorders, not just attachment.

Family Attachment Narrative Therapy targets each of the three spheres with parent narratives (see Figure 1.2). Claiming narratives target disruptions in attachment and relationships. Trauma narratives help children to process life events and the negative conclusions that were drawn about those experiences. Developmental and successful child narratives teach children and help them grow up. The importance of narratives and how they affect the inner working model is discussed below.

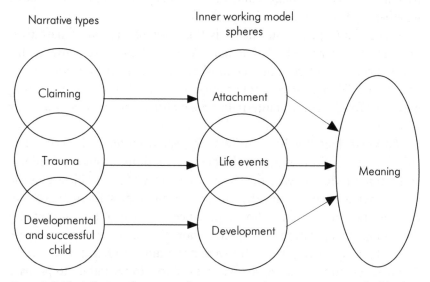

Figure 1.2: The influence of narratives. Parent narratives have an impact on each of the three spheres that make up the inner working model, ultimately facilitating change in the meaning a child has made of their life experiences.

The inner working model is a mental model of self, others, and the future based on the meaning a child has made of his experiences. This model begins to develop before the child's first birthday and is made up of emotions, sensations, and perceptions (Siegel 1999). During this implicit stage of memory development, attunement with the parent is primarily nonverbal and physical in nature. Parents connect and communicate with children through sight, sound, and touch. As the child begins to use language to communicate with the parent, a more explicit form of memory is possible containing facts and events as well as emotions and conclusions. The parent's words provide the framework for the child's experiences and memories. Narrative memory refers to the way experiences are stored and recalled in story form.

Words are used to enrich connections between the parent and child. As parents talk about the day, they have the opportunity to communicate understanding of the child's perspective and label his emotional state. As verbal communication between parent and child develops, an autobiographical, narrative self emerges (Siegel 1999). In simple words, he can now tell someone who he is and talk about what he has done, is doing, and wants to do in the future. It is by the use of narratives between parent and child that children learn cultural roles and expectations, the reasons for behavior, and the consequences of deviating from the cultural norm. This process is crucial for the development of conscience. The child must have internalized the beliefs and values of his parents in order to judge whether a particular action is acceptable.

Siegel (2001) suggests that it is this co-construction of narratives between parent and child that helps the child to make sense of his internal world (thoughts and feelings) and external world (environment and others). We believe parent narratives can provide the verbal meaning necessary for the child to internalize a new life perspective, a new inner working model.

So what does this have to do with peanut butter and a crib? The child's inner working model influences perceptions, thoughts, feelings, and actions. It defines who the child is. The story of Emily illustrates the importance of accurate, healthy inner working models. Emily was left at the hospital after her birth. She experienced the loss of her mother and the trauma of separation. She spent a short time in an institution where she had multiple caregivers who were not attuned to her unique needs. Traumatized and confused, she was moved to a foster family to prepare her for an adoptive family. Her experiences in this family are not known.

At the age of eight months she was escorted to the United States to join her new family. Again she experienced loss and trauma.

Emily's new family joyfully greeted her. At last, she had consistent, nurturing care by parents who were attuned to her cues. She laughed and smiled. She liked to be rocked to sleep and cuddled. When she was older, it got harder for her parents to put her to sleep. They would rock her to sleep but when they tried to put her down, she would wake up and cry. Well-meaning family, friends, and their pediatrician told them that she would never learn to fall asleep on her own unless they let her cry it out. Her parents took all the advice and did what they were told was best for their little girl. For a week they rocked her, read her stories, and then put her in her crib to sleep. She screamed and cried. They talked to her from the door of the room but did not pick her up. She eventually fell asleep sobbing. Again, she experienced loss and trauma. This little girl survived three life events considered traumatic to children. Once in her new family, she and her parents began to reconstruct a life narrative that was positive and coherent. She began to believe she was loveable, valuable, and her parents would always be there to take care of her. The events of the crib changed that belief. Now, for those parents reading this thinking, "Oh no, I did that when my child was a toddler," relax. Emily's previous attachment experiences and life events, her unique combination of prenatal experience, genetics and temperament merged to form her belief system. This belief system determined her interpretation of being left in the crib as a culminating event that came to define who she is. The frame of her inner working model was set. Each time she heard "no," was not given what she wanted, or was frustrated by failure, her model became more firmly entrenched. She started screaming in the crib, but now she screams in the car, the kitchen, the school, the bathtub, and everywhere. "No" means "I don't love you, I won't take care of you." At the age of 13 she stands screaming in the kitchen for her mom to put peanut butter on her toast. When Mom is busy and asks Emily to do it herself, she collapses on the floor crying, "You don't love me! You never take care of me!" The anxious, frightened toddler in the crib screaming to be rocked becomes the anxious, frightened teen screaming for peanut butter.

Robert believed the world was unpredictable and dangerous. When the police took him away from the house he didn't protest. With his heart racing, he silently watched out of the car window and kept an eye on the men on the front seat. The teddy bear they had handed him as they carried him to the car lay unnoticed on the floor. After they arrived at the hospital, he spent two hours in a room with lots of people bustling around. Some stopped to talk to him, or examine him; one gave him food which he shoved quickly into his mouth before it could be taken away. Eventually, he was back in the car. It was dark. This time they stopped at a house. It wasn't his house. A woman put him in the bath and then dressed him. He lay in bed with his eyes closed until the house seemed quiet. He slipped out of bed to explore. He would not sleep until he had figured out where stuff was.

Summary

The roots of difficult behavior in children can often be traced back to early attachment, life events, and delayed development. Children deprived of a nurturing, attuned relationship early in life with a caregiver tend not only to construct a chaotic life narrative but also form mistaken, destructive conclusions about personal value and the meaning of experiences. Fortunately, children also possess the ability to embrace an alternative or the deserved ideal, and construct new narratives. The key to constructing adaptive life narratives is discovering the child's inner working model.

Chapter 2

Putting the Pieces Together

Discovering the Child's Model

And now you ask me through your tears,
The age-old question unanswered through the years.
Heredity or environment, which are you a product of?

Robert's adoptive parents are at the end of their rope. Bill and Karen are committed to being his parents but lately feel like they should be committed. After successfully raising biological, foster, and adoptive children, they believed that they could help Robert, now four years old. They have parented many challenging children, but he seems to thwart every effort. The screaming, hitting, kicking, and spitting don't faze these parents. Their primary concern is his almost obsessive focus on getting what he wants, when he wants it. Bill and Karen describe how Robert sneaks out of his room at night to play and to get food. When confronted he denies it. When put back in his room he begins screaming and chanting to get what he wants, keeping the whole house awake. They give in to restore peace but feel angry and resentful. Their home is being run by a four-year-old. He behaves like the perfect child when anyone else is around but as soon as they leave, he starts manipulating to get what he wants. "How can he be so good at it? He's just four! What's he going to be like when he's 13?" Karen who works at home is the most discouraged. Despite her best efforts to love and nurture him, nothing has changed in the 14 months he has been with them. No consequence or punishment seems to matter and they have tried them all. Bill and Karen end the story by asking: "Why does he do this? How can we help him?"

The success of Family Attachment Narrative Therapy rests on discovering the meaning the child has drawn from early life events and evaluating the effect of these experiences on the child's development and ability to handle future stress. Although children usually enter our program with multiple mental health diagnoses based on their behavior, the "why?" of the behaviors is different for each child. Many parents contact our clinic stating that they have seen a "RAD symptoms" list on a website and that their child displays many of these behaviors. For many parents this is the first time they have been able to name what is going on with the child. Finding a name is a relief, as is knowing that there are other families out there struggling just as they are. However, a child with these behaviors may not have a disorder of attachment. We have evaluated children who exhibit few or none of these "symptoms" and yet displayed patterns of attachment behavior that might be categorized as insecure. We have also assessed children who displayed every one of these symptoms and yet do not have reactive attachment disorder (RAD). A solid diagnosis of attachment disorder must include an evaluation of the child's early life history and of the quality and strength of the current relationship between parent and child.

A 12-year-old girl was referred for treatment after being evaluated by another professional and given diagnoses of oppositional defiant disorder and reactive attachment disorder. During the process of determining the meaning of her behavior the team discovered that an older brother had told her she was adopted. Subsequently a series of events took place within her family that indicated to her that she was being treated differently and unfairly. Her behaviors matched those from the list of symptoms commonly associated with attachment disorder. But her early history did not match criteria for reactive attachment disorder. Her behavior appeared to be a deliberate attempt to break the emotional connection between herself and her family. When her mistaken beliefs were discovered, loving birth narratives along with actual videos of her birth shifted her inner working model and restored the relationship between her and her parents.

Caution must be used when comparing a child's behavior to a symptom checklist. A review of research failed to reveal a link between these behaviors and current research on attachment patterns. Some behaviors on a checklist may be closely related to disorganized/disoriented attachment (Gurganus 2002). However, it is the pattern of interaction between the child and others that reveals the nature of the inner working model, not just behavior alone.

The goal of discovering the inner working model is not searching for the correct diagnosis. Diagnostic labels in children are generally descriptive of behavior and tend to be unstable, changing frequently depending on the current situation and the diagnostician's bias. There is a place for diagnoses. There are times when a diagnosis suggests a particular type of treatment. A mental health diagnosis is often necessary to receive financial, therapeutic, or educational support. But the label itself is less relevant than the information that leads to it, information that helps in understanding the child.

Applying a diagnosis to Robert's behavior may be the first step in developing a treatment plan in many traditional therapies. He most likely would meet criteria for reactive attachment disorder and oppositional defiant disorder (ODD). Some might classify his symptoms as childhood bipolar disorder. He is also displaying behavior that could be related to ADHD (attention deficit hyperactivity disorder) and has some obsessive-compulsive features (OCD) as well. It's quite an alphabet soup but these diagnoses reveal little about the meaning of the behavior. The key is to focus on the underlying issues: what happened to Robert in the spheres of attachment experiences and life events and at what developmental level is he functioning? This information along with discovering the beliefs about his experiences will shape the stories that lead to healing.

Family Attachment Narrative Therapy assumes that behavior is symptomatic of deeper underlying issues. Without addressing these issues the behavior cannot permanently be changed. Discerning the meaning of behavior in children with attachment problems is a crucial step in the healing process. The child's history and current behavior will provide many clues to the inner working model, and discovering the meaning of this information is vital to effectively address the child's problems. This chapter discusses how parents can discover the child's inner working model.

The search

Managing behavior and establishing emotional bonds isn't enough. Effective treatment for children requires discovering the child's inner working model. Bowlby (1973) suggested the internal working model could be understood by knowing the detail of the events in the life of the child. The single most important source of information about children with disturbances of attachment is the parents. By living with the child and observing her behavior, moods, preferences, and all the individual peculiarities associated with their child, parents possess the specific knowledge needed to make sense of the behavior. Parents can research early history, notice behavior in the home, school, and community, and seek out objective and projective testing if necessary. At this point, many parents may be thinking, "If I knew my child so well, I wouldn't be reading this book! I don't understand her at all any more." Living with children or adolescents with attachment issues is not easy. Previous experience just doesn't fit this child. Nothing seems to explain his or her behavior and nothing seems to work. It's complex and it's a mess. But parents really do have clues and information that can help piece it together.

Discovering the inner working model of a child usually takes time. While a simple "I'm bad" may characterize some children's beliefs about themselves, other children present with a many faceted belief system. Somewhat like Sherlock Holmes, parents go down many dark alleys to collect clues and evidence, unsure of what the final solution to the mystery may be. But, like any good mystery, part of the intrigue is in the endless possibilities. It is sometimes challenging and always fascinating.

History

Our first consideration is the child's early history. The question of "what happened to this child in his/her early years?" is asked of all parents and professionals involved. What kind of care and nurturing did the child receive? Were there multiple caregivers? Were the child and caregiver separated? For how long? Was the child in daycare? Were there any significant events that could have caused the child to conclude that caregivers cannot be trusted? We attempt to get as much background and history as we can on each child applying for admission into our program. We request birth records, medical records, police and child protection reports, social histories, placement and transfer summaries, and court documents. Previous psychological evaluations, school assessments, language, sensory, neurological evaluations all provide pieces to the puzzle. For some children volumes of records must be waded through and for others there is only a paltry amount of information. As we look ahead to treatment, collecting history on the child not only provides information about the development of the child's inner working model but also provides the content of the stories which will be used in Family Attachment Narrative Therapy.

Bill and Karen have very little documented history on Robert. Social services became involved when he was two-years-old after a neighbor called stating there was a child wandering around in the dark. When the police determined where he lived, they found the home full of garbage and animal feces. The toilet was overflowing and there was moldy food on the counters and in the refrigerator. The only adult present was his grandmother's boyfriend who had been drinking. Robert was transported to the hospital for an examination and then to a foster home. Both Tanya and her mother said they wanted him back. A reunification plan was set up but they did not follow through and the social worker began the process to terminate Tanya's parental rights. Robert was in foster care for five months before being placed with Bill and Karen, who hope to adopt him. He displayed many of his current behaviors in the previous foster home. Bill and Karen have additional information about his birth family and home from the foster parents who supervised visits with his birth mother Tanya and sometimes picked him up at the home. Tanya reportedly paid little attention to Robert during the visits. He watched TV or wandered outside by himself. He was typically returned with a wet, soiled diaper. Robert didn't have much of a medical history. Tanya had not followed through with check-ups. He had been seen in the emergency room for a head injury. The note said he had fallen down the stairs. He also had scars on his arms that looked like teeth marks.

Standardized testing

Testing may help parents describe their child's behavior, personality, and development. Testing can also provide important insights on how well the child is functioning, how they learn and process information, and how they perceive themselves, others, and the world around them. Behavior rating scales expose patterns and the frequency and intensity of behaviors. Parents who consult professionals find that each usually has his or her favorite instrument. We currently use the Achenbach Child Behavior Checklist (CBCL) (Achenbach and Rescorla 2001) and the Child Behavior Rating Scale (CBRS) (May and Nichols 1997). These checklists provide descriptive data in a standardized format. Specific features of the child as reported by the child, a parent, and teacher are compared to normative samples of peers. Again these descriptions are helpful but not necessarily diagnostic. Other behavior scales that may be helpful are the Conners' Rating Scales or the Behavior Assessment System for Children.

The CBCL provides information on a wide range of behaviors related to anxiety, depression, social problems, thought problems, attention, withdrawn, somatic, delinquent, and aggressive behavior. This checklist is helpful as we consider underlying feelings related to the child's maladaptive behavior. For example, many children with an anxious attachment have a high need to be in control. They attempt to control adults, peers, and all aspects of the environment, and may quickly blow up when that control seems threatened. A high score on the anxiety scale may suggest that insecurity and fear foster the controlling behavior. So trying to "out control" children may actually increase their fears and intensify their demands and anger. Why is the child anxious? What events could have caused the anxiety to develop? How is that anxiety manifested in his behavior with his parents? These are some of the questions that might lead to a hypothesis about the inner working model.

The CBRS is designed to assess the presence of behaviors that meet diagnostic criteria for conduct disorder, oppositional defiant disorder, attention deficit hyperactivity disorder, as well as behaviors that are typical of children with reactive attachment disorder. These are behaviors commonly reported by parents and professionals who work with children with attachment disturbances. The CBRS yields sufficient information to compare a child's functioning with diagnostic categories of mental health disorders. The CBRS also assesses the frequency and intensity of problem behaviors. As such, the CBRS is a useful intake instrument that can be used to screen children for potential admission into a treatment program. The CBRS can also document functioning prior to treatment and at various stages during treatment to gather data on treatment outcomes.

Children deprived of parental encouragement and support may have delays in gross and fine motor skills, speech, cognitive, and emotional development. These deviations from normal developmental abilities may be uneven. The child may be operating at his chronological age in verbal expression (he can talk the talk); however, when stressed, his ability to solve problems plummets to a level that is incongruent with his age (he can't walk the walk). The Vineland Adaptive Behavior Scales assess personal and social functioning of individuals from birth to adulthood (Sparrow, Balla, and Cicchetti 1984). The Vineland assesses behavior in four domains: communication (receptive, expressive, and written); daily living skills (personal, domestic, community); socialization (interpersonal, play and leisure, coping skills); and motor skills (gross and fine). It gives both standard and age-equivalent scores. Age equivalents are helpful as parents attempt to understand their child's difficult behaviors. An age equivalent of two years and eight months in the area of coping skills explains much to parents who are dealing with a 12-year-old's tantrums. The Vineland typically reveals delays in one or more domains of functioning for children seeking our help who have had a disruption in attachment or a traumatic life history.

A good illustration of the relationship between development and behavior is a ten-year-old adoptee who was living with his father and siblings. To avoid a court-ordered out-of-home placement after breaking and entering charges, he was referred for intensive therapy. The court was determined to send him to a juvenile correctional facility to deter future criminal activity. His Vineland revealed that he was operating at an 11- to 13-year-old level in the daily living skills area. To those who didn't know him well, he appeared competent − as if he knew exactly what he was doing. However, his expressive and receptive communication scores were in the five to seven year range and his socialization scores were in the three to five year range. His silence, interpreted as defiance by the judge, may have been due to his inability to comprehend what the judge was saying. His problem behaviors were in part due to low coping skills. He handled frustration and problems like a pre-schooler. He lost his temper and hit others and destroyed property. When he wanted something he took it. Being sent to a juvenile facility would not only contribute to his existing problems but would probably not deter him from the same behavior in the future. The Vineland revealed that he lacked many of the skills necessary to control his own impulses.

Other measures which may be helpful in figuring out why children behave the way they do include projective drawings, sentence completions, and projective assessments such as the Thematic Apperception Test, the Children's Apperception Test, and the Rorschach Inkblot Test.

Cognitive testing such as the Wechsler Intelligence Scale for Children and Stanford-Binet Intelligence Scales may provide information about the child's strengths and unique challenges. If prenatal exposure to alcohol or drugs is suspected, an evaluation for fetal alcohol syndrome or effects may be indicated. In addition, children who have experienced deprivation in the early years of life may have sensory integration problems that contribute to their misbehavior. If a child seems unwilling to accept affection from parents, it would be important to determine if this was due to an avoidant attachment style or tactile defensiveness. Assessments to rule out sensory integration dysfunction may provide additional information about the "why" of certain behaviors. The knowledge gathered through assessment is valuable to parents and professionals when there are pieces missing from the puzzle.

> Bill and Karen hoped that an evaluation would help them figure out what was going on with Robert. He was so different from any other child they had parented before. The results of some of the testing forms they filled out confirmed that he indeed was not just an active child. The Vineland ranked Robert low on the communication domain. He had difficulty understanding what was said to him and telling others what he wanted. His social skills were low too. He was not able to consider anyone else's needs, share with others, or give instead of just take. With this information it now made sense that Robert resorted to tantrums when he was frustrated. Bill and Karen also realized that their expectations for Robert were too high. Robert, however, was very independent and insisted on taking care of himself. He had a high score in daily living skills. It was easy to understand why Bill and Karen and his preschool teacher had treated him like other four-year-olds.

Observational methods

Observations of the child in play with the parent or with a therapist also provide information about the child's inner working model. Unstructured play time permits observation of the quality and content of play without imposition of outside limits. Following the child's lead, playing what she plays, doing what she does, while watching and listening can be fascinating. The emotional content of the play may reveal aspects of the child's inner working model. A child hiding under furniture, disguising herself, and burying figures in the sand may indicate anxiety and fear and even provide clues to how she handled her traumatic past and currently responds to stress. Noting general themes of symbolic play may hint at the conclusions the child has drawn about her life experiences. For example, constant battles in which opponents are overcome by brute force may reveal a belief in the need to be violent in order to survive. Keep in mind that there might be many reasons the child is fighting battles during play time. If it is a clue to his model, it will fit with the other pieces of the puzzle parents are collecting.

Play clearly exposes developmental delays. A 17-year-old who plays dress up, an eight-year-old who lines up cars moving them back and forth without an imaginative narrative, a six-year-old playing alongside someone else without interacting or sharing are all illustrations of play that might be considered developmentally inappropriate. For experienced parents, comparing the child to other children that they have parented in the past may help them determine at what level the child is functioning.

Observations of the parent and child playing together or structured observations such as the Marschak Interaction Method (Jernberg and Booth 1999), the Strange Situation (Ainsworth *et al.* 1978), or another separation-reunion task may be useful. The nature and quality of the attachment relationship between the parent and child is often revealed in their play and interactions together. The separation-reunion procedures can be useful in determining attachment behavior patterns in the child. Securely attached children confidently explore the playroom, check in and make frequent eye contact with the parent. In addition, there is a mutual enjoyment of the play and of each other. Attuned parents are attentive to the child's actions and emotions during the play and have age-appropriate expectations. Conversely, children who perceive that their parent is not physically or emotionally available may loudly object to separations, cling to the parent even in a room with inviting toys, avoid direct contact, disobey the parents' requests, refuse help or nurturing, and ignore the parents' comings and goings. The Marschak Interaction Method allows clinicians to assess how the caregiver structures activities for the child and whether he or she encourages engagement and completion of the tasks at an appropriate level for the child's development. They also reveal how playful, nurturing, and attuned the parent is to the child's emotional state and level of frustration.

Bill and Karen had lots of toys in the house and in Robert's room. He dumped them out, carried them around the house, and even threw them when he was mad, but he did not play with any of them. He didn't seem to care if a toy was lost or broken. During Robert's evaluation he was observed both with Bill and Karen and with a therapist. Robert always separated easily from Bill and Karen to go with the therapist. He did not talk much during play observations. Robert randomly picked toys off the shelves, played briefly with them, and dropped them to move on to the next. When the floor became cluttered, he just walked on top of the toys. He did not look like he was having fun. During the parent–child observations, he avoided eye contact and physical touch unless Karen offered food. He did not protest when Bill and Karen left the room or react when they re-entered. He was oppositional to Karen's requests but would comply if Bill restated the request more firmly. Robert allowed a story to be read to him but immediately slid off their laps and stepped on Karen's feet. Parents report that if they had attempted this at home he would have been much more aggressive and loud.

What the parents know

Each child is unique. No therapist can ever understand a child's nuances at the same level as a parent, and this is precisely the type of intimate knowledge that is necessary to create effective narratives. Parents are able to describe in great detail the child's behavior and mood shifts – what makes the child tick. More importantly, the parent knows, or at least is in the best position to guess at, the underlying feelings and meaning of the child's behavior. Parents often possess stories and undocumented history that has been passed by word of mouth from previous foster parents or social workers. The child may tell her own stories as she becomes more comfortable in the new family or perhaps to shock or test them. ("Will you still love me if you know the worst about me?") The child may recall memories of traumatic events. However, some trauma may have occurred before the child acquired language skills and therefore the child cannot tell the story of "what happened back then?" In this case, it is her daily behavior that provides clues to what her experiences may have been. Children who have experienced abuse may flinch and raise their arms to protect themselves when parents move too quickly. They may fear baths, the dark, going to bed, or physical touch. Everyday stress or parental requests may result in flashbacks, hysterics, tantrums, or nightmares. Many experiences may remind them of where, when, and how they were abused. A child's action or reactions can provide information about possible traumatic events.

One four-year-old girl screamed hysterically when her foster mother ran water for the bath tub or backyard pool. Once the water stopped running, however, she happily played in the water. It was a mystery why. One day when talking about water, the little girl simply added one word: "deep." With a little encouragement other words and phrases were added: "shower," "door shut," and "grandpa." Her mother and a social worker who had known the birth family for years were able to piece together that she had once been in a glass shower stall with a man while the running water got deeper and deeper. The mother now had a better picture of a traumatic life event that had happened to her little girl and was able to craft a healing story to help her overcome her fears.

Bill noticed that if he moved too quickly, Robert flinched and ducked. When their older children had friends over to play, Robert usually retreated from the noise and activity. He watched but seldom joined in. When Robert first came to live with them, he could fall asleep anywhere. He would just drop off in the middle of bright lights and noise. He wandered out of the yard despite repeated consequences. Robert would go into the rooms of Bill and Karen's older children and go through their things, taking what he wanted. Sometimes he took money, but sometimes he just took junk that he couldn't possibly need. It didn't seem to matter what they said or did; he just kept doing it until they finally put locks on their doors. When Bill and Karen considered Robert's history in relation to these behaviors, the behavior began to make sense to them. All of these behaviors served a purpose in his previous family.

Relating behavior to the child's history can be a painful process especially if the parents have been reacting to difficult behaviors with anger and consequences. Many parents feel guilty about the "less than perfect" techniques they previously employed once they understand the behavior. Putting the behavior in the context of the past touches the parents' empathy for the child and stirs up anger at who and what caused their child's pain. It also suggests new ways of dealing with challenging behavior. Instead of just reacting to the behavior, parents have an opportunity to become an understanding champion of the child. As parents begin to understand why the child is doing what she is doing, hope is renewed. Now they have a way to help the child heal and give themselves relief from problem behaviors.

Embarrassed by frequent phone calls from her daughter's school, one mom worked hard to shape up the out-of-control behavior. As she discovered the meaning of the behavior, however, her approach changed. Now her goal was to help the school understand why her daughter behaved the way that she did. The school provided services to special needs children. Kids were frequently pulled from class by professionals in white lab coats for occupational, physical, or speech therapy. In the orphanage, the medical director wearing a white coat took sick children out of the group. Some never came back. Her daughter was terrified of being taken. It was not bad behavior; the specialists were triggering a traumatic memory.

One of the most common problems parents seek help with is tantrums. Robert has loud and sometimes violent tantrums that disrupt the family and limit their activities in the community. They never know when he is going to "go off." Bill and Karen have heard that sometimes the child is taking out all his or her past anger on the new, "safe" parents. That may be true but it doesn't make them feel any better. When asked what usually triggers the tantrums Karen reports that usually it's when Robert doesn't get what he wants, when he wants it.

What is underneath Robert's powerful drive to get what he wants? How did that need develop? How is it related to his prenatal environment and his early history? Have his early attachment and trauma experiences affected his development? How do these delays affect his ability to learn and to handle stress? Bill and Karen, along with the professionals assisting them, were not able to answer these questions outright. However, they had some hunches, and were able to make educated guesses based on what they did know and on intuition. Many of the answers were contained in the stories they told about Robert.

Karen states that last week she put Robert in his room to cool off during a tantrum. He kicked and beat on the door as usual. She can see his room from the kitchen and keeps an eye on him as he will sneak out and try to get whatever it was that he was mad about. Surprisingly he stayed in his room this time, maybe because it was close to naptime anyway. Karen walked by his room listening occasionally to make sure he wasn't destroying something. It was too quiet. She peeked into the room. He had pulled all of the covers off the bed onto the floor and was lying on top of the bare mattress rubbing his face against it. She notes that he seems to like rubbing things on his cheeks. In a sing-song little voice he was repeating, "Nobody loves me and I don't care, nobody loves me and I don't care." Looking for the "why" of his behavior, Karen speculated that he might have been left alone a lot and rubbed his cheek to comfort himself. She reflected on this as she comforted him. She now had information that might be helpful in a narrative.

Discovery

There are key questions that lead parents and professionals away from behavior to the "why" and the "how." Why is the child behaving this way? How is it related to his early attachment experiences? How is it related to trauma in his past? Is it due to some deficit in his growth and development? The collection of stories and observations about a child contain pieces of the inner working model and may lead to healing narratives. The focus must always be on "what is underneath the behavior?"

After gathering sufficient information, the pieces can be put together to form a working hypothesis of the child's inner working model. The hypothesis should be constantly updated as new information is available. Narratives that target and shift the mistaken beliefs of the model are then possible. Often the child's inner working model can be characterized as "I am bad or evil, I deserved to be abused, I deserve to be hated, and my bad behavior is who I am." The model may be blatantly obvious. Hearing the beginning of a claiming narrative, "When you were a tiny baby you deserved to be loved," one child immediately began screaming, and frantically chanting, "No! I'm not! I'm bad!" But for other children, the meaning they have constructed for their life and future is deeply buried under layers of hurt, shame, and anxiety. The thoughts and feelings are unspeakable. Those around the child may only see difficult behavior. An interpretation based only on the external behaviors may obstruct the construction of potential healing narratives. How hypotheses are used to construct stories that help children connect, heal, and learn is discussed in the following chapters.

The formation of Robert's unique inner working model was profoundly affected by prenatal events. Unwanted and uncared for, his development was affected by his birth mother's alcohol and drug use. Once born he was left alone and had few loving interactions with the adults around him. Anger changed to despair. Some infants might have died, but not Robert. He had determination. He was a survivor and once Robert was mobile he found ways to get his own needs met, to comfort and soothe himself. Unrestricted, needs merged with wants. Developmentally delayed, he had few words to express himself, poor impulse control, and limited cause and effect thinking. Robert was four, yet Bill believed that Robert thought he was an adult, free to come and go and do as he pleased. Bill and Karen's stories about Robert provided pieces of information that helped them make sense of Robert's tantrums and other behaviors. He seemed to believe that he did not need anyone. He used adults to get what he wanted. But adults were not to be trusted. He felt safer if they just left him alone. As their understanding of Robert's inner working model grew, their frustration with him decreased. Bill and Karen intuitively knew that they would need to make a connection with Robert before they could use narratives to shift mistaken beliefs and conclusions that fueled the behavior.

Summary

Behavior cannot be permanently changed without addressing underlying attachment, trauma, and developmental issues. The "why" of behavior is different for each child. Parents are the primary resource for information about the child. Testing and observation may also be helpful. The goal is not to find a diagnostic category but instead to discover the child's inner working model. The search is for the meaning of behavior. Parents and professionals seek to understand the relationship between the behavior and the child's early attachment experiences, life events, or development. Once a hypothesis is formed, narratives are constructed that target the negative and erroneous conclusions formed in early childhood. New beliefs develop that can change the child's inner working model.

Chapter 3

Narratives that Bond, Heal, and Teach

The first one gave you life. The second one taught you to live it.

The flames of a warm fire gently light the faces of a father and daughter cuddled under a faded star quilt. Entranced, the child listens attentively. She turns the pages as her father reads the story that has become their nighttime ritual. She wants the same story to be read over and over again, eventually memorizing the words and "reading" to Dad. It's one of those moments that you hope the child will treasure forever.

Story time is a perfect bonding activity. Bonding activities are any actions that increase physical proximity and facilitate feelings of safety, security, affection, and trust. It is a time when emotional connections are formed between two persons. Reading stories, playing games, mealtimes, bath and bedtime rituals, holiday traditions, and simply spending time together are examples of bonding activities.

The parent of a child with attachment disturbances and behavioral disorders may have a different experience of these activities. The child complains, interrupts, wiggles, and fidgets before hopping off to go play with something else. So much for the moment to treasure. Some parents have compared it to cuddling with eight pairs of elbows and knees. They are left with feelings of frustration and disappointment rather than closeness and intimacy.

Family Attachment Narrative Therapy can be an effective tool to help children develop trust, heal from past experiences, and learn new behaviors. The key is discovering the child's inner working model and meaning of the behavior. Then narratives are constructed to address the negative belief system that drives the behavior. Generally parents begin with claiming narratives, stories which assist the parent and child in developing an emotional bond and a feeling of belonging to the family.

Eventually narratives are introduced to address the child's trauma history, problem solving, developmental delays and growth, teaching of empathy and moral behavior. Parents also use narratives to impart family values, faith, history, and rituals. As we evaluate the narratives we have heard over the years, some common themes emerge and these will be presented in this chapter. Narratives represent the ideal in parenting; what it could have been like for both the parent and child had they been together. Narratives never attempt to alter the child's actual history. Instead the child is introduced to new possibilities for positive beliefs about self and others. The narratives convey the parents' unconditional love for the child. Stories work. Parents can help their children heal through this powerful medium.

Section 1: How Narratives Work

Words have the ability to shape our thoughts, feelings, beliefs, actions, and relationships. When placed together in a cohesive form such as a story, the effect can be more powerful. Stories instruct us and help us make sense of our experience of the world. Stories allow readers to see themselves connected to the past, present, and future (Siegel and Hartzell 2003). Readers will take on the perspective of the hero or main character if they can identify with it.

Any lover of the fine arts is familiar with the capacity of a story to affect an individual's thoughts, feelings, and subsequent actions as vividly as if that person were actually involved in the experience. Some authors use the power of a story in their work to alter conceptions. For example, after an encounter with two children whose mother had gotten rid of the family pet as a punishment, composer Paul Schoenfield wrote a piece of music to assuage the pain the children were experiencing. Called *Dog Heaven*, the piece tells the story about a jazz club in Dog Heaven, a place where the streets are lined with bones and there is a fire hydrant on every corner (Schoenfield, undated).

Jerome Bruner (1987) suggests that life narratives have the ability to organize memory and perceptions, and give purpose to life. Our stories become who we are. Narratives also may allow for "continuing interpretation and reinterpretation of our experience" (p.12). Our stories change over time and with new experiences. We believe that parent narratives can help the child internalize a new life perspective, a new inner working model. An individualized story told by parents who intuitively know their child's needs and emotions offers a way to renew the mind of the child. Negative and faulty meanings in the child's ongoing life story can be changed. As she identifies with the hero of her parents' story the little girl feels understood. She's not alone any more. There is someone else like her. In addition, empathetic and attuned interactions during story time correct her existing beliefs about parents.

The core belief of Family Attachment Narrative Therapy is that the parents can help children heal from past negative attachment relationships, traumatic life events, and the resulting developmental issues. Our methodology has been challenged, extended, and refined by the parents we have worked with over the years. Creatively utilizing narratives in ways we hadn't imagined, we as professionals have found ourselves following their lead and expertise in helping their children. The basis for this expertise was parental attunement. Empathetic understanding of how current problem behavior related to the child's past and level of development guides the corrective stories that can change negative inner working models.

The importance of parental attunement

Emotional attunement is the foundation for all secure attachment relationships. When parents are attuned they seem to have an inner eye and ear for the child's thoughts, feelings, needs, and desires. For example, a mother playfully copies the facial expressions and sounds of her infant until he becomes overwhelmed and looks away. The mother reduces the amount of stimulation until her baby indicates with eye contact, gestures, and gurgles that he is ready to play again. A father, hearing the familiar five o'clock whine of his toddler, puts aside the day's mail, and snuggles with him, touching, talking softly until his son hops up to fetch a toy. Each of these parents is demonstrating attunement to their child's cues.

Temperament and early life experiences make each child unique. As new parents become acquainted with their child, whether a newborn or an older adopted child, the meaning of her nonverbal cues such as facial expressions, posture, and movement becomes clearer. Eventually they are able to read her signals and anticipate her needs. Many parents excitedly anticipate holding, rocking, singing, and playing with their newly adopted infant. In these quiet moments the bonds of love begin to grow.

But what if the infant spent the first months of his life alone in a crib? When Tyler arrived at the airport with his escort from the orphanage overseas, he did not look at his parents, smile, or respond to their attention. He lay limp and lifeless in their arms. Those special moments they had waited two years for were silent and eerie. His mother knew she had to bring this child back to life. She bounced and danced and twirled and sang loud, silly songs to him. She stroked him, tickled him, and gently coaxed him back into the world. Soon Tyler was laughing, mimicking his mother's facial expressions, holding his head up and sitting alone. Intuitively, his mother had provided the essential sensory stimuli needed to heal his past neglect. Eventually, quiet rocking and cuddling became a regular nightly ritual and promoted a strong emotional connection. The road to healing and attachment was the innate attribute of this mother, not the result of professional education and training.

Infants naturally demonstrate attachment behaviors such as smiling, babbling, crying, and reaching out. When the parents respond to those behaviors by smiling back, cooing, soothing, and touching, the child's social-emotional development is enhanced. The first year is a critical time in which infants are discovering who they are and organizing strategies to relate to others. When attachment behaviors work, she tries them again and again, not only with her parents but also with her big brother, aunt, and the neighbor down the street. The expression on her parents' faces tells her who she is. "I'm special, important and loved."

When parents are consistently attuned and available to the child, the relationship will evolve into a cooperative exchange. During the first months of a child's life, the responsibility for initiating and realigning attunement lies with the parent. If the parent misses the cue the first time, it is important to try again. As the child develops language and cognitive skills, however, there is a move toward a more reciprocal relationship. Older children are able to consider the needs and wishes of the parent. They begin to give back. A securely attached child notices the parent, initiates interactions, and becomes an active partner in the relationship.

After doing narratives intensively with her adopted daughter, one parent reported that her daughter offered her baby blanket to her when she was lying on the couch recuperating from the flu. She was shocked, as her daughter is usually very needy and demanding when Mom is sick. For the first time she had noticed her mother's needs.

Without the experience of attunement in infancy, however, the child cannot move toward that goal-corrected partnership (Bowlby 1969/ 1982, 1980). For parents, it feels as if they give and give and give, yet cannot fill the child's insatiable needs. They get nothing from the child in return except more demands and more arguments.

Attuning to the older child

How can parents have an emotional connection with a child who seems unable or unwilling to accept love and care because he experienced neglect, abuse, and abandonment by another parent? How can parents be expected to understand and empathize with behavior that can be violent and seems hatefully directed at them?

> Renee needed special shoes to help her ankles develop appropriately. But the shoes were ugly and different from the shoes her friends wore. She deliberately rubbed a hole in her new shoes hoping she wouldn't have to wear them ever again. Renee's mother could have speculated that the deliberate destruction of property was due to an underlying anger and rage. That hypothesis might have led to a logical consequence such as earning enough money to replace them. Was Renee angry about having to wear the special shoes? Yes, but that misses the underlying thoughts and feelings and leaves Renee feeling misunderstood and still angry. Instead, Renee's mother understood her daughter's motivation. As she was attuned to her feelings, the special shoes were replaced. She had to wear them but, in addition, she received a coveted pair of black patent leather shoes to wear to church and other special occasions. Renee learned about respecting property and the relationship was enhanced by the exchange.

We believe parents possess an innate ability to successfully care for and nurture their child. The biological, physiological, and neurological systems of parents are designed to care for children. Some adopted and foster children experience attunement in the first year of life. They may be able to verbalize or organize their behavior so adoptive parents can achieve attunement and meet their needs. But children who did not experience attunement as an infant may not have developed an organized or effective strategy to relate to others. That deficit leads to ineffective and even bizarre behavior in the parent–child relationship. Despite adoptive parents' best attempts to respond to their child's cues, they miss the mark.

It would be easy to misinterpret David's behavior. He wanted his dad to spend more time with him instead of watching TV after work. When dad's brand new leather recliner arrived from the store he stabbed it repeatedly with his pocketknife. A weird way to say, "Play with me Dad!" Dad was understandably furious. When a child has an attunement deficit he is not capable of a goal-corrected partnership. He cannot see or understand his parents' needs and instead is focused on getting his own needs met. When an attuned parent disciplines a securely attached child, the child may protest and argue but ultimately trusts and understands that the parents' discipline represents their love and desire to protect. Without this partnership and without an attachment to the parent, requests and appropriate parental interventions appear punitive and unfair to the child. These mistaken perceptions reinforce the child's negative inner working model.

Daniel Siegel (2001) proposes five basic requirements for fostering secure attachments: *collaboration, reflective dialogue, repair, coherent narratives,* and *emotional communication. Collaboration* is the experience of sharing nonverbal signals such as eye contact, gestures, facial expressions, tone of voice, and body language. As the parent and child exchange nonverbal cues and adjust their responses contingent on the other, there is a profound feeling of connection between the pair. This is clearly demonstrated when a mother mirrors her infant's sounds, facial expressions, and movements. She allows her to lead the dance, increasing the intensity of her reactions in response to her excitement and soothing her when excitement and glee evolve into agitation. Siegel suggests that such collaboration is essential in developing a sense of self. The parents must also verbally communicate to the child their sense of the child's internal experience in a *reflective dialogue.* This allows the child to attribute meaning to the experience. Verbal narratives accompany the nonverbal communication that takes place within the mother–child dyad. In the example given earlier, the mother matches her tone and intensity to her infant's cues as she narrates her inner state. "What a happy baby you are! You like kicking your strong legs. Mama's watching you. What a big smile! Oh, it's OK, Mama's right here, you're OK. You just scared yourself, didn't you? Mama's here, Mama's here." Sometimes cues go unnoticed or are misread, and the internal state of the child is not responded to or incorrectly communicated to the child. The parent must then re-attune or *repair* the connection to the child. While running errands, a mother misses her toddler's signs that she is tired and a tantrum over something minor occurs. Rather than giving her over-whelmed daughter a time out, she instead cuddles her close, softly reas-suring her, "You are so tired, aren't you sweetie. It's OK, we're going home soon. We'll find your blanket and rest." When adults join the child in constructing stories about past, present, and future, the child is able to integrate her experiences and to form a *coherent narrative*. Day-to-day chatter remembering the morning's trip to the library, talking about lunch as the peanut butter is spread, and planning what to do after naptime are examples of how a parent might narrate a day in the life of the child. Reminiscing about past events, telling the story with a begin-ning, middle, and end, also helps the child make sense of her world. Parents who reflect their child's emotions to her facilitate the child's ability to identify and express feelings appropriately. "Your face looks mad right now. What do you need?" "Can mama help?" These are examples of *emotional communication* that is attuned to the inner state of the child and helps the child understand that her emotions are acceptable.

All five of these elements are present in Family Attachment Narrative Therapy. During the storytelling the parents pay attention to the child's nonverbal signals. They may mirror or reflect those signals and feelings in their voice or facial expressions or incorporate them into the story. One child immediately made the connection between himself and the character that was telling "big fat lies." He looked away and squirmed. In response his mother lowered her eyes and head, illustrating how the character in the story looked away from his parents and fidgeted in embarrassment. Then the fictional parents encouraged their son that he could and would make the right decision next time. Parents may also adjust the content, pacing, and length of the story based on the child's reactions during the telling. For example, shallow breathing and increased muscle tension may indicate that the topic is painful or scary and parents may respond by revealing less detail about the event in the narrative or by touching and cuddling the child closer to them. Parents also help the child make meaning of her experiences by attributing to the protagonist the thoughts, feelings, and perceptions they believe are similar to the child's own internal experience. If they believe the child feels that her birth mom "gave her away" because something was wrong with her, then the character in the story has the same belief and feelings.

The parent repairs any misunderstandings or miscommunications based on the child's reactions to the narrative. After an emotional narrative about a child's grief when she was placed in foster care, a 12-year-old told her adopted mom that she could not remember her birth mother doing anything with her. She said she missed her mom a little but not her old life because there was nothing to miss. Another child disagreed with her parent's statement that the hero was scared when she was locked in the closet and said, "No, she liked it in there. Nobody could see her." If the narrative has "missed the mark," adjustments can be made later in the story or in the next telling. Many children will correct any misperceptions during the story, allowing the parents to immediately integrate the new information into the narrative. Finally, the telling of what happened to the child in the past, and what may happen in the future, facilitates a coherent narrative. Throughout the process parents include both factual information and emotional communication. Through voice, facial expressions, and other nonverbal signals, they communicate that they share the child's hurts and the joys. The parents name emotions for the child and reassure her that all feelings are valid.

Goal-corrected partnerships are difficult to achieve until the deprivation of attunement has been rectified. Family Attachment Narrative Therapy provides a way for the parents to convey that they know and understand their child's experience of neglect and abuse and the mixture of confusion, terror, sadness, and rage their child may have felt during it. The parent accomplishes this by using narratives to bond, heal, and acknowledge the various ways the child used acting out behavior to try to control or make sense of the past and the uncertain present. The parent also needs to explicitly name and challenge the faulty, destructive conclusions about self, others, and the environment. The focus is on renewing the child's mind so that the emotional connection necessary for growth can occur.

Summary

Problem behavior in children is often the result of negative, self-defeating inner working models. Parental attunement to the child is a necessary requirement of successful Family Attachment Narrative Therapy. Empathy and caring for the child allows parents to see the child's irritating or even frightening behavior differently. This ability to see into the mind of the child helps parents understand the meaning of the child's behavior. Discovering the inner working model assists parents in developing realistic expectations for the child. Knowing the meaning of behavior guides the development of narratives.

Section 2: Constructing and Telling Stories

Some readers might be thinking, "This isn't going to work because I can't tell stories." We would argue that answering the question "How was your day?" *is* telling a story. Many conversations between two people contain a story. Whether a simple illustration or an elaborate, epic tale, children love stories. As the narrative is constructed, attunement to the child's inner thoughts, feelings, and motivations guides the process. The child's day-to-day caregivers are most attuned to the child; therefore, the best narratives will come from parents. The following pages describe the elements of a good story, how to create a warm setting, and how to make a story come to life for the child.

The setting for Family Attachment Narrative Therapy

How can parents of older adopted or foster children create moments that bond, heal, and teach? These moments of quiet and openness can be few and far between in the normal everyday life of work, carpools, and household duties. In addition, children with attachment disturbances and behavior disorders behave in ways designed to anger and push away adults, especially parents. After months, even years, of rejection, parents may be resentful, hurt, and reluctant to engage in activities that may leave them vulnerable. Parenting children with extreme behaviors leaves parents and children upset and both may just want to be left alone. Attunement facilitates emotional receptivity to the bonding feelings aroused in Family Attachment Narrative Therapy. However, in order to achieve attunement it is necessary that parents make themselves vulnerable again. A better understanding of the child's inner working model and the meaning of difficult behaviors enables the parents to take the risk. Knowing the child's life story may uncover long buried feelings of empathy for the child.

Both the parent and child must feel safe in order to enter into a state in which they are vulnerable to one another. For some families, narrative work must be done in a neutral place such as a professional's office. The support of a knowledgeable, empathetic therapist may give the parents the encouragement they need to make themselves vulnerable to their child. At home, parents can put aside a special time each day and create settings in which the parent and child will be most receptive to attuned interactions. A room free of distractions and with comfortable seating, soft lighting, and familiar comfort items such as blankets and stuffed animals may help the child quiet and relax, enabling her to accept the parents' emotional and physical nurturing. The child is invited to sit close to the parents or on one of their laps. In some cases children will refuse to sit near their parents. Safety and comfort are necessary for the success of the narratives. Holding the child is not. Many parents have successfully used narratives with resistant or very active children.

> A five-year-old boy moved continually during the narrative; from lap to lap, between his parents, on the arms of the couch, behind the couch, and he even laid across the back of the couch, smiling at them like a Cheshire cat. Discouraged, the parents attempted the narrative later in the day, adding new material, hoping to interest their son. They were surprised when he exclaimed, "You didn't say that part before." Despite his activity, he had not missed a word they said.

The parents may also encourage the child to look them in the eye and may gently remind their child throughout the narrative to maintain eye contact. Mutual eye gaze creates pleasurable states in both mother and child (Schore 1998). Eye contact seems to facilitate deep emotional connections. The parent and child "see" and know the mind of the other. If the child has difficulty making eye contact in this setting, power struggles should be avoided. As both the child and parent become comfortable with the process of Family Attachment Narrative Therapy, the amount of eye contact usually increases.

Appropriate touch is important too. Shared physical gestures of affection provide a multi-sensory experience of each other. Of course, parents must take into account any factors that might contraindicate touch, such as sensory integration issues or unresolved sexual abuse. Parents may stroke their child's face, run their fingers through the child's hair, or massage lotion on her hands or feet. Children may respond to this nurturing by reaching out to play with their mother's hair or explore her face. In this setting, parents may also find themselves relaxing and enjoying the closeness with their child. The synchronized dance that takes place between them as each alters their attention, stimulation, and emotional level in response to cues from the other results in a resonance (Schore 2001a), a state of "feeling felt" (Stern 1985).

Incorporating props in the telling

Some children need concrete objects in the telling of the narratives; other children may be distracted by them. Parents can usually predict whether or not props will enhance their child's experience with narratives. Children who have been institutionalized, neglected, or abused often have difficulty understanding what they see and hear. A child with auditory processing problems or poor short-term memory for verbal information may benefit from incorporating visual props. Enlisting a family of dolls, stuffed animals, or matchbox cars as the main characters in the story may keep the child interested and attentive. The parent or child can draw pictures to illustrate important parts of the story. Keep in mind that if it appears that the child is operating at an earlier emotional or cognitive stage of development, he may enjoy props or toys that are appropriate for a much younger child. Even adolescents may need to see and touch the baby layette which parents would have bought for them. Parents of an adolescent girl adopted as a preschooler picked out a beautiful infant dress, pink (her favorite color), with lace and ruffles and black patent leather shoes. She was tickled with the purchase and keeps it with other mementos from her childhood. For children who are in the developmental stage of concrete operations (Piaget and Inhelder 1969), props may transform the abstract thoughts and feelings of the narrative into a concrete, realistic representation. A handmade blanket, special stuffed animal, baby rattles, bottles, pacifiers, and toddler's blocks and trucks can make the narrative come to life.

One mother brought her child to the baby department of a local store, showing her all the things she deserved to have as a baby. Her foster daughter had never seen a bassinet, walker, baby swing, and the other baby gear available to parents today. She was amazed as she walked down the aisle gently touching the articles. She continued to ask "Would I have had that?" questions for weeks.

In designing the setting for Family Attachment Narrative Therapy, Bill and Karen purchased a double rocker so that all three of them could comfortably participate. They chose a room in their home that could easily be de-cluttered in order to decrease the distractions and sensory stimuli. Recognizing Robert's anxiety and hypervigilance, they carefully placed the lights to dispel shadows. Karen provided pillows and blankets around the room in anticipation that Robert would not sit on their laps for long. Although he had difficulty tolerating close physical proximity, they felt certain he would continue to listen to the story even from behind the rocker. Because he often rubbed his cheeks on the bed and floor, they bought a soft, velour baby blanket for him. A bottle with his favorite juice, baby lotion, and a few baby toys completed their purchases. They were ready.

Creating a story

Stories have the potential to change lives. Constructing a narrative that will shift the child's negative inner working model is a challenge. For some parents, making up a healing, bonding, or teaching story for their child seems like an impossible task. "I'm not very creative," "I won't know what to say," "I'm not very good at telling stories," and "I don't think I can do this" are thoughts and feelings shared by many parents endeavoring to learn something new. We believe that storytelling is a natural way to communicate. In most cases, with a little instruction, support, and encouragement, parents have the ability to tell a story that touches the child's heart and mind. Appendix B contains a story construction guide or worksheet that parents may find helpful as they consider and choose the elements of the unique story they are designing for the child.

Parents are very aware of their child's learning style and language skills. Vocabulary and sentence structure vary in relationship to the child's age, developmental level, and expressive or receptive language skills. Parents can adjust stories for a perfect fit. In the case of international adoption, English may be the child's second language. Translators may be used in the telling of narratives. Parents may also incorporate vocabulary from the child's first language into the narratives. During a two-week intensive at our clinic, much of the work done by a child's parents was in the child's native language in which the parent was fluent. Although the therapist learned some words and short phrases by the end of the treatment, for the most part she was unable to understand the narratives told by the parents. This intensive was highly successful, reinforcing our belief that parents are indeed capable of helping their children with Family Attachment Narrative Therapy. They are the agent of healing, not the therapist.

We have listened to thousands of narratives over the years. There seems to be three common themes, which run through each of the four types of narrative: *claiming, trauma, developmental,* and *successful child.* These themes appear over and over again regardless of the child, the child's inner working model, or who is telling the story. Because they reoccur so often, we believe they are an important factor in shifting the child's negative beliefs. These themes are as follows.

- From the first, you deserved to be loved and cared for by parents you could trust.

- Even though you experienced abuse, abandonment, or neglect you deserved to be loved and cared for by responsible parents.

- Your behavior does not define your value and I (we) will be there to love and support you as you make changes.

The perspective

Choosing the perspective in which the story is told is an important component of story construction. In a story told from the first person, the protagonist is the teller of the story. The events happen to her. The thoughts, feelings, and conclusions drawn are her own. "I looked around for my mother but she was gone" is an example of a first person statement. The first person perspective is often used in claiming or developmental narratives. For example, in relaying family history to a child as part of the claiming process, a father talked about the adventures of his own childhood. He humorously conveyed the message that a child deserves love even when his brother leaves him stranded on the top of a barn and his dad has to get him down with the front loader. In developmental narratives, parents may use the first person to describe how they struggled to learn a new skill as a child. As a result, children know that their parents understand something of the difficulties they face.

In a story using a third person perspective, the teller describes events, feelings, and characteristics of other people. The protagonist is someone other than the storyteller. Pronouns such as "she," "he," or "it" are commonly used. Third person narratives are useful in many situations and are typically used in trauma and successful child narratives.

A story told from the third person is useful to discuss events in the life of a child when all the facts aren't known. The child's history on a day-to-day, moment-to-moment level is unknown. Third person narratives allow parents to recount what is known along with what is supposed. For example, if medical records indicate that the child was diagnosed as failure to thrive, parents could conclude that the child might not have been fed every time she was hungry or that at times there was no food in the cupboards or refrigerator. Although that might not be totally accurate, the story allows the child to process related memories, thoughts, and feelings. Third person trauma narratives are also useful in discussing difficult material and protecting the child's fragile feelings for her birth family. Adopted or foster children are bonded to their birth parents. Despite what happened, it was their mom or dad. They are loyal to them. Even children who did not know their birth family often develop a fantasy of what that family is like and develop feelings for them. It is important to respect that bond. It is not necessary for those bonds to dissolve, or for the child to be angry about what happened back then in order to develop a connection to new parents. Saying "Your birth mom left you alone in the crib" often results in an immediate denial, "No she didn't!" The third person story allows the child to maintain her relationship to her birth parent. At the same time, parents can present the facts in order that the child can begin to process those events and make sense of her life story. Third person narratives also give the child a zone of safety. She is free to keep the story in the realm of "just pretend" when the content is difficult. This ensures that the child is not being re-traumatized by the telling of the story. This is discussed in further detail in Chapter 5.

Talking to a child about her behavior may be like talking to a brick wall and certainly won't create warm fuzzy feelings between parent and child. Telling a child a story about an interesting character with similar problems builds the relationship while teaching new behaviors. The use of third person successful child narratives allows the child to listen to behavioral alternatives without becoming defensive.

Sarah was severely neglected as an infant and appeared to have some sensory integration problems. She seemed unaware of where her body was in space. As a result, she intruded on the personal space of her peers and family. Circle time at school invariably ended up with Sarah in tears because someone had pushed or hit her after she practically sat in their laps. Mom and Dad told a creative narrative about "bubble aliens." Touch one and everyone ends up covered in green, yucky slime. Sarah laughed about the aliens' antics, but got the message too.

The hero

Finding a hero to whom the child can relate is one of the most critical parts of story construction. If parents are successful in doing this, they communicate to the child that she is understood and the child is more open to receiving the story's message. The stronger the identification between the child and a story's hero or protagonist, the better the child will be able to internalize the message of the story. As the child internalizes the message, adopting the perspective of the protagonist, her own inner working model is challenged. The new perspective must either be integrated into the old, shifting the faulty meanings the child has previously fabricated, or discarded and the old model retained.

The hero can be anyone or anything with which the child will identify. Television, movie, sports, and cartoon characters from the popular media may be used. Sometimes a make-believe child with similar problems will work. In addition, some children have a particular animal with which they are fascinated. Dinosaurs, dolphins, stray puppies, and tigers can be used as the main character. If the character and the situation hits too close to home the child may react defensively. On the other hand, if the situation is too dissimilar and identification doesn't take place, the message may be missed. Attuned parents are usually able to make this determination. But if the child doesn't connect with the hero, a simple change of characters in the next telling usually does the trick.

The message

The content of the story is specific to the task at hand and determined by the child's unique inner working model. Narratives can be used to challenge the child's negative belief system. Stories that introduce an alternative meaning have the capacity to change the inner working model and, consequently, the life of the listener. Answering the question "what message do I want to convey through this story?" provides the blueprint from which the story is constructed.

Every good story has a beginning, middle, and end. The beginning introduces the main hero and the setting in which the action or plot takes place. Details about the protagonist's appearance, personality traits, and the setting help the child visualize the story during the telling. What color is the hero's hair and eyes? Does the action take place in the city, a forest, or on a mountaintop? After framing the backdrop in which the story takes place, the plot is the heart of the narrative and relays the message of the story. In claiming narratives, the plot may elaborate on the care the child or character deserved to have as an infant and young child. Trauma narratives relate life events in a coherent fashion and describe how the negative inner working model may have developed. The plot of developmental and successful child narratives may teach a skill or new behavior. The actions, thoughts, and emotions of the hero as he or she faces a dilemma or crisis hook the listener and build interest and suspense. Lastly there is a resolution to the crisis, which brings the emotional energy of the listener to a calmer state and usually holds the message of the story. Children traumatized early in life typically have difficulty constructing a narrative in this form. They have difficulty considering alternatives, making cause and effect connections, and resolving conflicts. By constructing a story with a sequence of events, a captivating plot, crisis and resolution, parents are able to teach their children about planning and form, not just content.

Bill and Karen decided to start with claiming narratives. They did not believe that Robert saw them as special to him in any way. They were just adults who might give him something he wanted. They also felt that if they started talking about what they would have done if he had been their baby, he would panic and have to either fight or run. For Robert this meant a tantrum or behaviors that would distract him from what they were saying. Bill and Karen decided to use a third person perspective in the claiming narrative. They would tell a story about another mom and dad who loved and cherished their brand new baby girl. Karen described how the mother took care of herself during her pregnancy so her baby would have a healthy start. Bill made screeching car noises when he talked about the dad speeding to the hospital. They showed Robert the blanket and toys the baby would have received from happy relatives and friends. He came close enough to touch the blanket. They told Robert how the mommy and daddy took care of the baby all day long and in the middle of the night too. They gave voice to the baby's thoughts and feelings as her parents nurtured her. How the baby stared at her mommy's face and grabbed her daddy's pinkie finger. They ended the story by describing the family's bedtime ritual. Karen even sang a lullaby. Robert wandered around the room and lay on the floor kicking the wall but he did not get angry and he did not leave the room. They kept it simple and short and felt pretty sure he had heard at least part of the story.

Summary

In telling stories that bond, heal, and teach it is important to create an environment as well as a story that promotes attuned physical and emotional nurturing. Parents and children who have been hurt and rejected have difficulty approaching any situation that exposes them to further pain. The storytelling setting must provide physical and emotional safety as well as invite openness and vulnerability. The surroundings at home or in a therapist's office should be quiet, with soft lights, and couches, pillows, and blankets. Props may be used to make the narratives concrete and believable. Emotional safety is generated through parental attunement. The child who feels understood is open to begin the attachment process with a new family.

Constructing specific types of narratives that make up Family Attachment Narrative Therapy is described in the next chapters. The examples given are designed to illustrate features of each narrative type. The best narratives are individualized to the child and told by the parent. Parental attunement, intuition, and hunches based on day-to-day interactions with the child are the key to constructing effective narratives.

Chapter 4

Claiming Narratives

The first gave you a need for love, the second was there to give it.

Imagine answering a knock at the door and being told by the adult waiting there that she has come to take you to a new home. The friendly woman states that it will be a forever home. Not only is there a new home and family but there is a new school too. It may take a while to meet new friends and learn the routine, she counsels, but it's for the best. This scenario is not far from the experience of adopted and foster children. In the case of international adoptions, some of this information may have been given by people speaking in a different language. The new home may be in a different climate, culture, and with people of a different race. The child may never see the same trees and flowers, smell the same smells, or taste the same foods again. Is this traumatic for children? Absolutely! However, the child's need for safety and a permanent family often outweighs the pain and confusion of change.

Being claimed by a family is extremely important to children who have been abandoned, abused, or neglected and moved from home to home. A claiming narrative establishes the rights of the parents of an adoptive child to provide physical and emotional nurturing. A claiming narrative establishes the rights of the child to belong, to be accepted, and to be cared for by loving, responsible parents. The word "claim" is defined by Webster's Dictionary (Collin 1999) as "to say you own [something] which was left or lost" (p.77). The experience of being accepted and belonging to a family is a basic psychological need. This feeling of belonging provides a secure base for children to learn, grow, and venture out in the world.

Section 1: The Purpose of Claiming Narratives

Claiming narratives can strengthen existing emotional connections or bonds between the child and family members, such as parents, siblings, and extended family. The narratives can also be used to pass on important family-specific information to the child, such as family traditions and history. Finally, in the telling of claiming narratives, parents may come to terms with issues such as infertility and relationship problems within their family of origin.

When parents find it difficult to bond

Adoptive or foster parents were not there when the child entered the world wet, slippery, and squalling. Connecting with older children is difficult. Connecting with older children who have been abused and neglected is even more difficult. The new parents did not cause the damage yet must deal with the behavioral and emotional fallout of the child's traumatic history. Parents are understandably angry about the child's difficult behavior and have struggled to develop an emotional bond toward a child who makes himself very unlikeable. Narratives allow the parents to experience the possibilities of what this child could have been like if he had received optimal, responsive care as an infant. Stories about "what it would have been like if…" allow parents to see their "challenging child" in a new way; as an innocent baby who from the first deserved to be cherished. Claiming narratives help parents see the child with fresh eyes. The child's loveable potential is revealed and behavior becomes just that, behavior. Separating the child from the behavior allows parents to empathize and provide unconditional love and acceptance.

When the child finds it difficult to trust

In claiming narratives, children experience the joy of being warmly accepted into existence. The love an infant deserves is not based on merit, but on the mere fact that he exists. Many traumatized children missed this unique experience, and claiming narratives provide an important opportunity to re-experience those moments, as they should have been.

Children who have their physical and emotional needs met by caring adults feel important and trust that adults will continue to be available, accepting, and responsive in the future. Children who have been abandoned and maltreated often assume they deserve it. Instead of trust they feel anxiety, shame, and anger. All children deserve a safe, loving upbringing. When the child hears that he deserved attentive, loving, responsive parents, it may be a revelation. Hearing what the parents would have done if they had been there when he was an infant encourages trust on the part of the child. Parents who use Family Attachment Narrative Therapy report that their children ask "would you really have…" questions for days and weeks after beginning claiming narratives. "Would you really have rocked me every day? Would you have really bought me these booties?"

Shifting the child's inner working model

For many children this is the fun part of Family Attachment Narrative Therapy. Hearing what it would have been like if they had been with this family from the beginning answers many questions and affirms their value to the new parents. Many relish the one-to-one time with parents and being the center of attention. They may even ask for the story over and over again. However, in some cases, hearing what it should have been like leads children to remember what it was like. Those children experience sadness and grief. One four-year-old slid off his adoptive parent's lap after the story and exclaimed, "What a rip-off!" He immediately recognized that he had missed out in his first family. And for others, being loved and cherished may be incongruent with the child's existing model of who he is and what he expects from the adults around him. Stories about what the child deserved in his early years may be met with resistance if the child believes that he is inherently bad and undeserving of love and responsive care from adults. It is not uncommon for us to see children covering their ears and refusing to listen to that "stupid baby stuff." Some try their best to destroy the mood and the moment. Each time one mother emphasized how she would have fed and cared for her preteen son if he had been with her from the start, he interjected statements like "yeah, I would have peed in your face!" or "and I would have barfed all over you." It was discouraging. She eventually discovered that he would tolerate stories about some other mom and baby and switched to the third person perspective. Over time, repetitive and consistent physical and emotional nurturing with claiming narratives can shift a child's negative conclusions about himself and the adults responsible for him.

Establishing birth order

Claiming narratives can be used to establish a child's place in the family. When a child enters the family, whether through birth, foster, or adoptive placement, a new hierarchy must be established among the siblings and roles adjusted accordingly. Conflicts may occur as the children work out this pecking order. Age is not the only criteria for arriving at a new order. Because children who are in out-of-home placements have often experienced multiple caregivers, trauma, and neglect, there may be delayed development in one or more areas. The new child may be chronologically older but physically smaller and emotionally like a much younger child.

> Scott and Mary adopted two teenagers from Russia. Tanya, age 14, and Nick, 12, joined Jill and Ben, their biological children. Jill was two months younger than Tanya. Ben was 13. Tanya and Nick had spent six years in an orphanage and experienced abuse and neglect in their birth home before that. Two years later Tanya has accepted her role, not as the oldest but as the third child. Both Jill and Ben will be going through driver's education before she does. She recognizes that she has a lot of ground to make up.

An older sibling sometimes shares in welcoming and caring for a new baby or child. In other cases, the new addition is not appreciated. Parents may choose to have siblings participate in the narratives. One family involved older sisters in claiming the adopted brother as their own by having them pick out baby things for him and presenting their new sibling with these keepsakes. Another older sibling told a newly adopted sister of her joy when she arrived, her love of the big sister role, and how she worked through occasional feelings of jealousy and competition. It came as quite a surprise to the adopted child that a birth child could be jealous of her. Sibling conflicts, hierarchy, and roles can be worked out in the telling of a narrative.

Claiming the extended family

The extended family is also involved in the claiming process when a child is born or adopted. There may be an endless stream of visitors after the arrival, all wanting to see and touch the newest member. Grandparents, aunts, and uncles often note the baby has Uncle George's ears and Grandpa Joe's eyes. These family characteristics, both physical and personality traits, are also important in the claiming of an adopted child. Many times there are remarkable physical similarities, but in the case of international or transracial adoption, the focus may need to be on how the child's sense of humor is like Aunt Martha's or how his mother loved to dance as a child too. Grandparents and other members of the extended family may take part in the claiming narratives as well. There is so much adopted and foster children don't know. Children of all ages enjoy stories about Mom and Dad when they were young. They are fascinated to hear that a great-great-grandparent fought in the civil war. And of course there is the all-time favorite of how far kids used to have to walk to get to school. Adopted children have years of experiences and history to catch up on. Claiming narratives answer the endless questions children have but may not ask.

Passing on the family traditions, history, and rituals

Faith and values can be transmitted in claiming narratives. Claiming narratives also teach a new child family history, traditions, and rituals. Inside jokes, pet names, rituals, and holiday traditions are strange, and for some, the differences are not welcome. Providing shared memories helps the child to feel as though he belongs to the family. Everyday dinner table conversation can be a mystery to the adopted or foster child. He does not have a shared history with his new family. Sharing the stories behind the family jokes helps the child identify with the family. A story about the time Uncle John and Dad almost drowned catching frogs explains the mystery of why everyone calls Dad "Kermit" at family gatherings. Parents may share their own life story, struggles, and joys in these narratives. Claiming narratives about the child's special role in holiday celebrations relays family traditions to the new child. How does the family celebrate birthdays? What will happen on the summer camping trip? Are gifts opened on Christmas Eve or Christmas Day? Will there be fireworks on the 4th of July? These questions and more can be answered in a claiming narrative.

Faith and values can be transmitted in family narratives. Descriptions of religious rituals such as circumcision or first communion can be included in the claiming narrative. Meaningful narratives have been constructed around how the family would have prayed for the child — prayers for normal development, safe arrival, protection, happiness, and prosperity. Parents who are committed to values such as giving to others, honesty, and integrity incorporate these principles into whatever narrative they may be constructing and telling (see also Chapter 7, Successful Child Narratives).

Other issues

For parents who have struggled with painful infertility or family of origin issues, Family Attachment Narrative Therapy can help heal those wounds. Claiming narratives, which incorporate events that occurred before conception and during pregnancy, may assist parents in processing the loss and grief of infertility. Couples have dreams about their future family. They envision themselves as a mother or father nurturing, teaching, and playing with the child. They dream of picture-perfect family holidays. They anticipate the loving feelings they will have for that infant. The loss of that dream is as real as a death. As the parent tells the older adopted child a story about their eager anticipation, the care taken during the prenatal period, and the joy of the first glimpse of that new person-to-be in the claiming narrative, both the child and parent share a healing experience.

There are no "perfect" parents. Most adults enter into parenthood with unresolved needs, losses, and even traumas. These issues may interfere with the process of attachment with a child. Claiming narratives describing children's early interactions with parents provide a model for parenting. The ideal parenting described in the claiming narratives helps them realize that if this child had been theirs from the very beginning they would have given him everything he deserved. Immersed in loving care and attention, they would have witnessed the child's full potential emerge.

> In the midst of a claiming narrative one parent realized that she would have wanted to be loved and cared for like this by her parents. Claiming narratives allowed her to re-parent herself. As she told her son about the love and nurturing he had deserved as a baby, the child within her was listening. In the telling, his possibilities became her possibilities.

The child's behavior also affects marriages, sibling relationships, and relationships with extended family, friends, and neighbors. When dealing with a challenging child, parents often feel isolated and unsupported by others close to them. Drawn together as a team through the narratives, partners begin to see and appreciate each other's strengths and characteristics. Siblings and other family members may choose to participate in the narratives. Understanding how the child's problems developed and realizing the potential of the child reawakens empathy for the child. Empathy reduces feelings of anger and frustration. Siblings, family, and friends again have the energy to support and help the parents.

Summary

When a child experiences abuse or neglect in his early years, he is at risk of forming a negative view of the world and the adults in it. Adults are perceived as unreliable, unavailable, and even dangerous. This world view or inner working model is applied to all adults in his life. Claiming narratives allow new parents to experience the child as their own precious baby. Narratives allow the child to experience the possibility that he deserved to be loved and cherished. The sense of belonging to the family is established by involving siblings and extended family, and sharing the family history. Attachment is strengthened.

Section 2: Telling Claiming Narratives

Claiming narratives begin the process of healing, attaching, and adjusting to traumatic life changes. Through narratives, the child begins to learn about the new parents, what he deserved as a baby, and what place he has in the family. Many children with attachment disturbances assume that the care they received from their birth family is "normal" and something all children experience. Some believe that rejection is deserved, because there is something wrong with them or because they did something wrong. In the claiming narrative the child's original life story is not being denied; instead, alternate possibilities are being presented. This begins the process of shifting those negative beliefs to a healthy model that will help the child begin to trust and feel secure in his new family.

If you would have been...

Good stories have an inviting setting, a protagonist or central character with whom the reader or listener will identify, a plot or dilemma, and a resolution. Start the claiming narrative by constructing the setting. Rich detail will add to the believability of the story and aid the child in visualizing the surroundings. Possible backdrops for claiming stories might be the birthing room at the local hospital or the baby's nursery at home. It may even be a room in the house on Maple Street where the parents lived at the time the child would have been born. Bonding may begin during pregnancy. If parents choose to start the narrative with the experience of being pregnant, the setting may be the doctor's office where they would have learned that they were pregnant or perhaps the romantic restaurant where Mom shared the news with Dad.

"Joshua, you know that you were in another lady's tummy and that we had to wait a long time to come and get you?"

"Yeah," he said.

"Well, we want to tell you a story about what we think it might have been like if we had been together from the beginning. You know we wished we could have come to get you sooner."

"Why didn't you?" Joshua asked. They have talked about this before but they answer each of his questions patiently.

"We had to fill out lots of paperwork and answer lots of questions. They wanted to make sure we would be the very best parents for you. When they finally said 'OK' we were on the very next plane to get you. But if we had been there from the very first, I would have cried when I saw you. Not because I was sad, but they would have been tears of happiness. You know I cry all the time, don't you? Then I would have counted your fingers and toes and kissed your nose. You were a beautiful, perfect baby who deserved to be loved from the start. Daddy and I would have held you close, looking into your beautiful blue eyes as we rocked you to sleep. You know the bassinet your sister used?"

"Uh huh," he mumbled.

"We would have wanted you right next to us so we could hear if you needed something. And the minute we heard you making noise, our eyes would have popped open and we would have been right there to see what you needed."

"Really? In the middle of the night?"

"Yep!" said Dad, "and there would have been a fight to see who got to feed you every time." Joshua's eyes sparkled with laughter at the thought.

"In the morning," Mom continued, "you would have had another bottle. Then it would have been bath time. I would put just a little water in that small yellow bathtub, you know the one in the attic. I would check how warm the water was with my elbow like my mother used to do. It would be nice and warm, not too hot, not too cold."

"Not cold, right?" said Joshua.

"Nope, my baby deserves clean, warm water for his bath. I bet you would have splashed water all over the floor and me!"

"Yep!" Joshua exclaimed gleefully.

"After your bath," Dad added, "it would have been play time. We would have put a clean, soft blanket on the floor and surrounded you with toys to look at and touch. We would have stayed right next to you, helping you grab them, teaching you how to hold on and shake your baby rattle. Then it would be time for another bottle and naptime. We would always rock you to sleep and be there when you woke up. You might be hungry again or you might want to play. Life is pretty routine and boring for little babies. Tomorrow we'll tell about what it would have been like if you would have had your first birthday with us."

The protagonist of a claiming narrative is "the baby." The child immediately understands that this baby represents him. He identifies with the baby. He experiences what the baby experiences with a new "baby like" wide-eyed openness. Children may intently watch their parent's face and gaze into their eyes. Often children ask questions and add to the story. It is not unusual for a child to ask questions directly related to his past history. For example, a child who had frequently been locked in a room for hours asked her new parents if they would have ever left her alone. Others ask if they would have had a certain toy or article of clothing. The child's identification with the protagonist helps him consider new possibilities. His view of self, the world, and the people in it begins to parallel that of the baby/child of the story.

In claiming narratives the plot is the story of how the child would have been physically and emotionally nurtured in this family. The child would have been loved, cared for, and protected. Many parents begin with pregnancy, birth, and infancy, followed by toddler and preschool years. The narratives may continue until the parents grow the child up to the age at which he did join the family. The narrative may focus on a holiday or special event such as baptism or a birthday. The story may incorporate the child's known background and history. For example, if the child was often hungry and ate food out of the garbage, it might be helpful to emphasize how he would have always been fed when he was hungry and given healthy food to eat. Children who have lived in a chaotic environment need, yet resist, structure. They often create familiar chaos in their new family. Hearing that they would have had bath time, mealtime, naptime, and play time day after day provides the consistency that was missed and teaches the new family's routine and expectations.

"Remember yesterday when we talked about what it would have been like if you had been with us from the start? If you would have been my baby back then, I would have baked you a cake shaped like a race car for your first birthday. We know how much you like race cars. Your room still has race cars on the wall, doesn't it?"

"Yeah and I have more race cars than anyone at school," Joshua piped in.

"Your sister would have wanted to blow your candle out for you. I would have let you try first but one-year-olds aren't very good at blowing yet. I would have funny pictures of you with blue frosting all over your face and in your hair. Grandpa and Grandma would have been at your party too and they would have given you a little race car that you could sit on and push with your feet. You would have made funny race-car noises as you raced around the dining room table."

"And you know," added Dad, "I would have had the video camera going the whole time. I probably would have given you a model race car but…since you were so little, I would have just *had* to put it together for you." Dad laughs, Mom groans.

"Joshua, half the toys you would have had would be ones that Dad bought so he could play with them!"

"What kind of toys?" Joshua asks.

"Well," said Dad, "first there would be the baseball and bat that you would have had before you even left the hospital after you were born. Then there was the football, the basketball hoop, the fishing pole, and the hockey stick. Boy, come to think of it, I would have had a lot of fun while you were a baby!"

"Tell me more, what presents would I get for my second birthday?"

"Remember Josh, you were with us when you were two," replied Mom.

"Oh yeah, so what did I get?"

"How 'bout we talk about when you came to our family in tomorrow's story?" asked Mom.

"OK," said Joshua.

Emotional attunement will help parents determine when the child is ready to leave story time. Sometimes it is as obvious as the child hopping off the parent's lap with "That's enough baby stories for today." At other times the child's emotional state and degree of relaxation will signal he is ready to stop. The ending may also leave the child wondering what happens to the protagonist next. What will he experience on his second birthday? Children typically look forward to story time. An adopted or foster child has faced many, many challenges; he may not have experienced many resolutions in his life. There is a satisfying ending to this story.

Be prepared for continued "Would you really have…" questions following the narrative. The baby food aisle at the grocery store, driving by the hospital, bath, and mealtimes bring questions to the child's mind. These questions, as well as the child's behavior between story times, give clues as to what the next narrative may need to cover. Nighttime insecurity may suggest a focus on bedtime rituals and mom's and dad's role in protecting children, while hoarding food may indicate the need for stories about the parent's role in satisfying the infant's needs.

Props and re-enactments are commonly used in the claiming narratives. Baby blankets, a baby bottle with the child's favorite beverage, baby toys, a massage with baby lotion will make the story come alive to the child. If the child resists any of the props or acting out the story, simply show the bottle and other items that would have been used if he had been born into the family to assist him in visualizing the experience.

Because of Robert's traumatic history and difficult behaviors, Bill and Karen sought the help of a therapist trained in Family Attachment Narrative Therapy to facilitate the attachment process. Robert had resisted most of their stories and nurturing efforts at home. In the therapy session, however, he smiled charmingly at the therapist and chatted happily. "I got new shoes on. See?" he said as he turned the lights in the room off and on again. "Do you work here? Do you have kids? My mom yelled at me yesterday. Can I have this [pointing to his mom's water bottle]?" He did not hesitate to climb into his parents' laps to listen to a story. As they started to tell him what babies deserve from loving parents, he glanced and smiled frequently at the therapist looking on.

"Robert," Karen began, "if you would have been our baby, right from the start we would have picked you up every time you cried. We would have never left you alone. When you were hungry we would have warmed a bottle of formula for you. Formula is like milk, only for babies. I would have boiled the bottles and the tops in hot water to make sure they were clean for you so you wouldn't get sick. Daddy would be the champion diaper changer in the family. Babies get a sore bottom if they are wet or poopy for a long time and we would keep you clean and dry." After a few minutes of the story, Robert became restless, moving and bumping awkwardly into them. Robert asked them to stop and said it was time to go home. He asked them questions about lunch and where his brothers and sisters were. He eventually got up and hid behind the couch. Initially exasperated and feeling rejected, Bill and Karen considered stopping. Underneath this resistance, however, they thought maybe he was nervous and uncomfortable. He wasn't in control. Instead of stopping they continued the story, holding a doll, and switched to a third person perspective.

"All babies are precious," Bill continued. "Babies need parents who are responsible. Moms and dads need to pay attention to what their babies need. Babies can't talk, you know, so parents have to watch the funny faces they make and listen for their cries."

Robert began chanting "I can't hear you!" and covered his ears. They finished the narrative despite the distractions. Throughout the remainder of the day, Bill and Karen made simple statements about other things that parents do to take care of babies. As Bill prepared dinner, he talked about how moms and dads put food into the blender to make food the baby can eat. As Karen helped him with a bath, she talked about special yellow bathtubs that babies need to be safe. Finally at bedtime when Robert had refused to sit with them for story time, they sat on the edge of his bed and talked about how babies need to be rocked to sleep each night and how music played softly keeps babies from feeling alone at night. In order to be in control, Robert needs to know everything.

Bill and Karen were banking on that fact and hoping that he was indeed listening. As Bill and Karen continued to tell claiming narratives in session and at home, Robert appeared to be distracted. However, they overheard him talking about the story with a boy down the street, confirming that he was indeed paying close attention. Karen gave him a hand-knitted baby blanket during one story. He immediately stated "This is a stupid baby blanket! I'm not a baby!" and threw it behind the couch. Bill later found it under Robert's pillow. Bill and Karen felt a glimmer of hope that their love for him was finally getting through.

Problem-solving tips

Not all story times together will be precious moments. At times the child will resist or behave in ways that make it difficult for the parent to even be in the same room with him. And life happens: older siblings need to be at soccer practice, there are bills to pay, appliances that flood basements, phones that ring; the list of demands that parents face each day is endless. Don't despair if problems occur, if the story seems lacking, and the child (or parent) seems bored. Try again and again. Some commonly asked questions about telling claiming narratives are addressed below.

I'm not very creative. What if I can't think of what to say?

Creativity is not a requirement for successful Family Attachment Narrative Therapy! Use past life experiences to build plots. If the parents have any past experience with infants and young children, they may draw upon that. Maybe they babysat as a teenager, or worked in the church nursery, or spent lots of time with a nephew; all those experiences can provide ideas about how the parent might have cared for a younger child. Words spoken from the heart are more believable and effective than scripts or reading books. Remember that it is the attunement between the parent and child that is most important, not the words that are said.

What if my child refuses to make eye contact with me?

Most children with attachment difficulties resist eye contact. We often think of eye contact as an intimate connection between two people, and this can produce anxiety in children who have come to expect only pain and hurt from caregivers. Eye contact will be even more difficult if a story has emotional content. Take care to not over-emphasize eye contact. It will naturally occur as attachment security and level of comfort increases.

If your child resists eye contact, determine the meaning of this resistance. Be sure to take into account the age and developmental level of the child. What feeling is behind the child's difficulty looking into the parents' eyes? The response to the refusal to make eye contact depends on what is driving the behavior. If it is fear, eye contact may improve over time. If it is a need to be in control, to not let the parent have power over him in any way, this may be addressed in future narratives. Story time should be pleasant and enjoyable for both the parent and child and not just another area for the child to engage the parent in a power struggle. Keep in mind too that some cultures avoid eye contact. So, your child's avoidance may have nothing to do with attachment whatsoever!

What if my child refuses to even sit on my lap?

Again, question what is the meaning of this behavior. The answer to that question will help decide what plan of action to take. Avoid power struggles. Perhaps the child will make some physical contact, rest his head on a shoulder, or hold hands. Dramatic facial expressions, a soft voice, and props may interest the child and draw him closer. We have had parents successfully tell stories to children on the couch, behind the couch, under a blanket, and on the floor. One child was not even in the same room and watched his mother tell a story to a doll on a video monitor.

My child tries to control the story. Should I let him?

Some children will ask questions and guide the telling as they attempt to answer questions about what their life would have been like with the family. In this case, including the information they seek in the narrative will satisfy their need to know. If the child controls the story to the point that the time together becomes adversarial, it may be appropriate to ask the child to wait until the end to ask questions or end the story time altogether for the day. Try to understand why he needs to be in control of the narrative. This awareness may provide direction for another story. For example, if he is trying to control the story time due to anxiety about doing something new and different, a future story plot may be about a character who is afraid of anything new.

My child always asks for cuddle time when I'm busy and then refuses when I try to do it later. Do I have to drop everything?

The inner working model for many children impairs their ability to trust adults. Being in control makes anxious feelings decrease. They seek to control the adults and environment around them at any cost. A set time for stories each day may give the child the structure he needs to feel more secure. When he asks, a simple reminder that cuddle time will be at 7:15 as usual may be enough reassurance for the child. For others, a parent's willingness to be flexible and meet the child's need sends the message that he is loved and special to the parent. Some children reinforce negative inner working models by setting themselves up to be rejected and then becoming angry when their requests for nurturing are not met. This is the child who has to talk about his abusive past the minute the phone rings. Or the child who demands a hug when a parent's arms are full of grocery bags. The response depends on assessing the meaning of the behavior. Putting down the grocery bags in the middle of the driveway to give him a hug may surprise him and lets the child know that he is more important than daily chores. If it becomes a pattern, the focus of future narratives may be to reassure the child that parents love him even when they are busy.

Summary

Claiming narratives begin to shift the child's dysfunctional inner working model developed as a result of his early attachment experiences. The parent conveys to the child that he is someone who from the first deserved to be cherished. Claiming narratives also help the child adjust to his new family. The child identifies with the main character in the story. The possibility that the child deserved responsible, loving parents becomes imaginable. Parents often report that their child appears happier, smiles more, and seeks out physical affection frequently during the period that they are telling claiming narratives. The parents' emotional attunement to the child helps them to find creative ways to deal with any resistance.

Chapter 5

Trauma Narratives

One sought for you a home she could not provide.
The other prayed for a child and her hope was not denied.

A common childhood fear is the loss of a parent through death or separation. This theme permeates children's stories and movies. Whether the movie is based on a classic tale such as *Peter Pan* or *The Jungle Book* or films such as *Home Alone* and *Finding Nemo*, the story often involves characters who have lost one or both parents. The plot unfolds, revealing their triumph over danger and search for love and family. This underlying and pervasive fear can sometimes be seen in children's play. Games such as hide and seek, peek-a-boo, and imaginative games where the children are lost and surviving on their own help children master their fears of abandonment and loss. This fear can also be seen in children's dreams and nightmares of their parent's death in natural disasters, being kidnapped or left behind. For many children, the trauma of danger and loss is part of their everyday experience, not just a fairy tale. Every year millions of children experience some form of trauma.

Section 1: The Purpose of Trauma Narratives

Every life is a story unfolding day by day, sometimes dramatic and sometimes ordinary. Many people wonder what their life would have been like if they had been born into another family, grew up in another city, married someone else, studied a different major, or had one more child. Every event in life changes the story. Sometimes the story is changed intentionally by a decision; at other times, a chance accident changes the course of life. Looking back, one can see how events, actions, and choices brought them to this point. But no one can go back and redo life. Or can they?

Children who have been abused or neglected often develop negative beliefs about life events and themselves. Looking back on their story, they see only a myriad of mistakes, misfortunes, predicaments, losses, and emergencies. They judge their life and themselves as "bad." Any "good" is forgotten or dismissed as chance. Van der Kolk (1996) has postulated that a person's fear response can be allayed by an attachment figure and by internal models of security. Trauma narratives can heal the child's old wounds; moreover, they can shift the child's negative inner working model. As the inner working model is changed, new behavioral and emotional responses are available to the child.

Healing the pain of trauma

Language utilizes and links many areas of the brain (Cozolino 2002). Because new experiences can change the brain, early negative experiences can be repaired. Growth and healing are possible. Narratives or stories may be used to reorganize the brain. Trauma narratives can be used to help a child recover from past abuse, neglect, and loss. The telling of the child's life story facilitates a reprocessing of the events and decreases distressing emotions connected to the events. As the child's life story is told in the third person narrative format, she can do the work of reprocessing without triggering fear or defenses. Many children can not or will not talk about their trauma history. In the telling of the trauma narrative, parents can open the door for discussions. Through the story they can convey their acceptance of the child no matter what, as well as their belief that what happened to the child was not her fault. All of these components help the child to heal. Children may express anger at the person who perpetrated the abuse one day and staunchly defend them the next. Or they may not talk about it at all. There is no single, right way for them to go through this process.

Shifting the child's inner working model

Trauma narratives can create new working models and shift the child's negative conclusions about her life story. In the telling of the story, the child's perspective becomes more realistic and judgments of the events more accurate. The child sometimes experiences genuine sadness about past losses. In the trauma narrative the child's love and loyalty to birth parents is recognized and the child is then free to separate the feelings about the birth parent from the feelings about the abuse and neglect she suffered. A child may love her birth parent but hate what happened. The child's feelings of shame and responsibility for the traumatic event often diminish. Effective trauma narratives can shift negative conclusions children have made about the event, themselves, and the adults around them. In our experience, this seems to happen spontaneously. Sometimes, a child will make a matter of fact observation like, "My birth mom wasn't very responsible but my new mom keeps me safe."

Creating understanding and empathy

In the telling of the child's trauma narrative, adoptive or foster parents often regain empathy for their child. The past is not used to excuse current behavior problems. However, hearing the child's life story again assists parents to put behaviors into perspective. A child who steals food, leaving the remains and wrappers stuffed everywhere, may be driven to hoard because of her background of malnutrition and neglect. This behavior is less irritating when the parents understand the meaning of the behavior. Telling and hearing their child's story also increases their understanding of the child's difficulty in trusting and attaching to them. Empathy for the child fosters bonding feelings. This empathy also helps parents become more attuned to their child and brings up feelings of anger toward the person who caused their child such deep pain. Children may be surprised and even pleased when parents thoughtfully express their outrage. Although criticizing the birth parent can be counterproductive, championing the cause of the child and what she deserved may give the child permission to feel her own anger, if only vicariously through the adoptive parent.

Empathy and understanding may also develop in children through the use of narratives. When the abuse was severe, children may numb themselves to both the physical and emotional pain. They may talk about intense, horrific trauma with very little emotion. Many traumatized children seem baffled when they observe others displaying strong emotions. This confusion may be interpreted as lack of concern and caring. One child laughed when she saw her mother and sister crying during a tragic scene in a movie. She didn't realize that her numbness toward the scene was strange, not the crying. As trauma is processed, however, some children regain their ability to experience emotions more fully. They may be able to experience a range of emotions such as sadness, loneliness, anxiety, and fear, as well as anger. As these emotions become integrated, children may begin to show signs of developing empathy and understanding for others. Because they have felt sad, children can recognize that feeling in another.

Summary

Traumatic events initiate a stress reaction in the brain as the child attempts to organize a protective response to the danger. When the trauma is the absence of a caring, nurturing relationship with the parent or another caregiver, the child may develop a negative inner working model of herself and adults. The child may see herself as bad, adults as untrustworthy, and the world as an unsafe and dangerous place. Trauma narratives heal the wound. Hearing the story helps the child make sense of what happened. In telling the story the parent can reassure the child of her innate value and that it was not her fault. Presenting the facts challenges the inner working model and leads to new conclusions. As parents develop and tell the story, behavior is put into perspective. The child develops genuine emotions and empathy.

Section 2: Telling Trauma Narratives

The telling of trauma narratives honors the life experience of the child. It's her history, how she came to be the person she is. In the arms of her parent, the child experiences herself as loveable despite her past. Although some children are able to listen to their trauma story and reprocess those events with apparent ease, other children are resistant. Not thinking about the events and not feeling the fear, sadness, and anger are effective defense mechanisms children often developed to protect against painful memories. Use of third person narratives may decrease the possibility of resistance or dissociation to the reality of the child's experience. When the storyteller utilizes the child's favorite animal, television, or sports character as the story's protagonist, the child's attention is captivated and the child is less defended against processing her own traumatic life events. Third person narratives also provide safety. The child can identify with the experience and emotions of the character yet maintain enough distance so that she does not become overwhelmed. Some children immediately recognize that this is their story and may say, "That's my story, so why don't you just use my name?" Others keep it in the "it's just a made-up story" category until they are ready to handle the content and feelings. Some children do not consciously recognize the story's similarity to their life at first. As the story is repeated, the traumatic material becomes less sensitive and children may begin to see the parallels to their own life.

Throughout the narrative, the message that the protagonist did not deserve what happened and that it was not her fault is essential. After selecting a character with which the child will identify, parents may begin by describing the setting and events leading to the trauma. Some trauma is prenatal and the narrative depicts what the birth parent(s)' life may have been like before the character appeared. Once the stage is set, the story is told. The amount and extent of detail revealed about the trauma depends on what the parents believe the child can handle in this first narrative. If parents are unsure how their child will respond, it may be wise to keep it simple and keep it short. Additional facts and details may be added in subsequent tellings. Parental attunement to the child will help them know when the child has heard enough or whether she is ready to assimilate more information.

The story content is often difficult to hear. Lack of eye contact, restlessness, and fidgeting may indicate some normal anxiety and discomfort. This is to be expected. The past is painful; but remember, she has already survived it. Recalling it with a safe and nurturing caregiver will not retraumatize her. Taking the child one step beyond her comfort zone helps her to begin to accept her past. Avoiding it may send the message that it is too scary, too shameful, and too bad to be brought out into the open. And again, the third person narrative allows her to examine the events and feelings from a safe distance.

Children may anticipate rejection when their new parents know everything about them. Weaving in the message that the child was not at fault and deserved something very different assuages these fears. Out in the open, there are no more shameful secrets. Experiencing unconditional acceptance from parents helps the child to accept the experiences and herself. New beliefs about herself take hold and strengthen, as the negative inner working model becomes obsolete and inaccurate.

"Instead of reading you a story, I want to tell you a story tonight, OK?" Mom asked. "It's kind of a sad story but it has a happy ending. Ready?"

Angie said, "OK," somewhat suspiciously.

"Once upon a time," Mom began, "there was a family of cats who lived on a farm in the beautiful countryside. The kittens lived in an old shed with holes in the walls and roof, and when it rained, they would get wet and cold. But they loved to play in the meadow on sunny days and chase butterflies. The mother cat was a very young cat and did not know how to take care of her kittens. The father cat was a big old alley cat from the city. Sometimes he brought the family big fat mice from the barn for dinner. But sometimes he drank bad water and he would get angry and even mean. He would snarl at the mama cat and swipe her nose with his claws. Sometimes the mama cat would run away and leave the kittens behind. They cried and mewed for her until the father cat hissed and swatted them with his claws. The little kittens were afraid and lonely but they learned not to cry. Sometimes the father cat would go away somewhere for days and then there would be no food for the cat family."

"Weren't there any people around to take care of them?" Angie asked.

"No, I'm afraid not," said Mom. "This family lived out in the country on an old farm and there weren't any people living in the old farmhouse."

"But why didn't the mama cat do something?" Angie interrupted again.

"Well remember she was a very young cat, almost a kitten herself. She didn't know how to take care of her kittens. Sometimes when she was running away from the mean old tomcat, she would find some other cats and stay with them. Because she was such a young cat, she would play like a kitten and forget to go home to her babies. But the little kittens were smart little kittens. Pretty soon they figured out how to find food on their own. They found bugs and worms, even grass to eat. It wasn't the good kind of food kittens deserve, but they survived. One day they left the shed to find food and wandered all the way to a town. Towns have lots of garbage cans you know. They thought they had found a feast. But it still wasn't the kind of good food they needed."

"Did the mama cat miss them? Did she look for them?" Angie asked earnestly. There was a tension in her voice.

Not sure what Angie needed to hear at that moment, Mom asked, "What do you think the mama cat did?"

In a very matter of fact voice Angie said, "I think she looked but she gave up too soon. Can we stop now?"

"Don't you want to find out what happened to the kittens?"

"Not right now, maybe later," Angie replied. The tension was gone from her voice so Mom let her go.

As the story is told and retold the child's anxiety and discomfort will subside. She will become more comfortable with the narrative. Sensing the parents' love and acceptance, the child may begin to reveal new details about the past, which are then incorporated into the story. The goal is not investigation; it is helping the child integrate these memories into her life story and shifting faulty, negative conclusions she drew based on those memories. Some children believe that they are protecting the new parent by not revealing their trauma history. Or they may be protecting their perpetrator. Accepting new information from the child in an empathetic yet matter of fact way signals to the child that adults can be trusted with her memories.

"Are you ready for another story, Angie?" asked Mom.

"Not the cat story again, Mom. I know that's just my story," said Angie in the "do it my way or else" voice Mom knew so well.

"It might be like your story, but it's about a bunch of cats, not a beautiful little girl. Who should the story be about tonight then?"

"How about a Barbie and Ken story?" Angie asked, feeling pretty sure this would start an argument.

"Are Barbie and Ken the mom and dad or the kids in the story?" said Mom, calling her bluff.

"The mom and dad, I guess," said Angie, knowing she wasn't going to get out of it but thinking maybe she could make it short like last time.

"Barbie and Ken lived in Malibu, in a pink house by the beach."

"Wait!" said Angie. "My mom and dad didn't live together ever!"

"This is about Barbie and Ken though, not about your mom and dad. The stories aren't exactly the same. I don't think they ever lived in Malibu either. Anyway, Barbie and Ken lived by the beach. It was a lot of fun for them. They could lay in the sun, play volleyball, go swimming, and have parties with their friends."

"See, this is going to be about me!" Angie tried again.

Not deterred, Mom kept going. "Now this Barbie and Ken aren't like the ones in your coloring books. When they had a party it got pretty wild. Sometimes the police would show up to tell them to quiet down so the neighbors could sleep. Sometimes they missed work because they were so tired from last night's party. If they missed work, there wasn't enough money to pay for stuff and then Barbie and Ken would get into big fights. Life went on like this for quite a while until Skipper came to live with them. By this time the house was getting pretty run down. Nobody cleaned; they just wanted to have fun. There wasn't always food in the house, there were lots of loud, noisy fights, and lots of parties. Skipper was pretty little so she couldn't take care of herself, or talk or walk. She could only cry and then Barbie and Ken would get mad and fight."

"I'm tired now, I'm going to sleep," announced Angie. Angie did not appear anxious or upset; Mom's intuition was telling her that this was more of a control issue.

"That's fine," said Mom. "Close your eyes and sleep while I finish the story. It's OK if you fall asleep. Anyway, as she got older she learned to find her own food. She liked to make Barbie and Ken and their friends laugh so she sang songs and danced dances, wiggling her hips like she saw the grown-up ladies do. Everybody smiled and laughed and called her their little princess when she did that."

"Stop talking, I can't sleep if you're talking!" Angie exclaimed.

"I'm almost to the end honey," said Mom as she began rubbing Angie's back. She could tell Angie wanted to start an argument but she knew she loved back rubs too and hoped that would settle her down. "Some days Skipper would wake up, and Barbie and Ken would still be sleeping. They slept most of the day after a party. Skipper would find something to eat and watch TV. It was boring. One morning she found the door open. Usually it was locked and she was too little to reach the door knob. She went outside and wandered down the beach. It didn't take long for her to realize that she was lost. She couldn't see the pink house any more. Skipper started crying. A nice lady stopped and talked to her and called someone on her cell phone. Pretty soon a police officer came. Skipper knew all about the police. They came to the pink house a lot. People ran out the back door or hid. She was scared of them. She told the lady that she lived in a pink house. The policeman put her in his car and drove just a little while until she saw the house. He took her in. It was a mess from the party. He looked around at the bottles and needles all over. He seemed very interested in the white powder all over the coffee table. He took her back to the car and used his radio to call someone. Then he went back to the house. Another police car came. This time a lady police officer took Skipper and put her in the other car. She was talking to Skipper as she drove away but Skipper wasn't listening. She was looking out the back window watching Barbie and Ken get in the other police car. She was really scared. She didn't know where they were taking her or what was happening to Barbie and Ken. 'How would they find each other again?' she wondered.

That's enough for tonight I think," said Mom. Angie was pretending to sleep and just made some noise. Mom was pretty sure she had heard the whole story. "I'll tell you what happened to Skipper tomorrow. Goodnight sweetie."

As discussed previously, children commonly dissociate from the strong emotions that may have accompanied their trauma experience. Intense fear, sadness, and hurt are too painful to feel for any extended period of time. When abuse or neglect is repetitive, children endure the incident disconnected from the emotion. Trauma narratives begin to connect the thoughts and feelings to the memories. The parent, as the narrator of the child's life, gives voice to the internal dialogue going on within the protagonist. If the child blames herself for what happened, then the character also blames herself. If the child might have been afraid, heart racing, body trembling, then the character experiences terror. Even though it may not be 100 per cent accurate, the child is reassured by the fact that another child had the same thoughts and feelings when bad things happened to her. Sometimes the child will correct you: "Nah, he didn't feel scared any more, it happened all the time."

Utilizing the inner dialogue, the protagonist models the healing process for the child. In the story, the character is loveable and valuable. Self-blame changes to understanding that the protagonist deserved something different. Anger changes to sadness, and then acceptance and moving on. The child identifies with the loveable character and may consider the possibility that her birth parent loved her despite the abusive behavior and irresponsible choices. Accepting that she is loveable, she also realizes that her new parents can love her. And if those parents can love her no matter what, maybe they are worth her trust.

Skipper's story might continue with Mom talking about the fear and confusion she felt as she was taken to a shelter home. The story might describe how she constantly thought about Barbie and Ken. Where are they? Are they in trouble? Why don't they come get her? Have they forgotten about her? Don't they want her back? The story might follow her journey to a foster home, on reunification visits, through the termination of rights process, to an adoptive home and finally to the courtroom where she becomes part of a new family. If Angie refused to listen to another Skipper story, which seems likely, the narrative would be just as effective if Mom picked up the story with a different cast of characters.

In a variation on trauma narratives, parents have used life books to help children develop a coherent life narrative. The life book is an ongoing autobiography of a child's life (Keck and Kupecky 1995). Pictures, videos, drawings, and mementos may all be included to tell the child's life story. The chronological discussion of the child's memories and of the book becomes a story with a beginning, middle, and end. The child may reveal more information about the past, but that is not the purpose of reviewing a life book. The goal is to help the child make sense of the past, understand how she got to the place she is now, and recognize future possibilities.

As a general rule of thumb, parents tell trauma narratives over and over again. Sometimes it is the same story; sometimes the setting and characters change and additional details are added. When a child has worked through and developed some mastery over the story material he may want to move on. If the child is no longer interested in any version of it, displays no emotion during the story, and no behavioral difficulties after the story, he may be done with it for now. Parents may revisit trauma narratives with their child again if he brings up new information, asks questions about his past, or displays behavior that parents believe is related to his traumatic experiences. As children enter a new developmental stage, for example moving from the stage of concrete operations to formal operations where they are able to think in abstract terms and consider hypothetical situations (Piaget and Inhelder 1969), trauma narratives may be used again. Hearing the story this time in a different developmental stage, the child is able to consider possibilities that may not have occurred to him before. Adolescents may ask difficult questions as they realize past events are not as black and white as they used to seem. The fact that his birth mom didn't know how to take care of babies was an adequate answer at six. At 12 he may want to know why she did not take classes to learn how to take care of her baby. At each stage of development, trauma narratives may help the child reprocess his earliest life experiences.

When to seek professional help

There are times when parents should seek a professional to help their child work through past trauma. Some indicators that narratives told at home may not be sufficient to shift the inner working model and change behaviors related to trauma include the following.

- Some children dissociate when memories of the trauma are triggered. As a young child, unable to escape the abuse physically, she may have discovered that she could escape psychologically and emotionally. Dissociation became her defense of choice. Now the child seems to "space out" in the middle of everyday activities. When something reminds her of what happened early in her life, the child automatically dissociates to defend against possible pain. Seeking a professional who has experience with dissociative episodes may be wise.

- Many professionals assert that parents should not bring up the past with a child who has been traumatized but rather allow the child to bring it up when she feels safe. Good advice in some cases, but every child is different. Some children will bury the memories, thoughts, and feelings. They are unable to understand the connection between their current anxiety, anger, and behavior, and the past. Trapped in the past, they do not develop an emotional connection with their current

caregivers or the skills to deal with the past events. When
defenses impair a child's ability to function in the family,
school, or community, professionals and parents can develop a
plan to help them face the past and thus move forward in life.

- The process of resolving past trauma is difficult for both parent
and child. At times problem behaviors intensify as the child is
working through her past. While most parents will not
experience any behavior more difficult than they have
previously, some prefer to have the support of professionals
during the work. If behavior progressively deteriorates,
professional help should be sought. If the child threatens to
harm herself or others, seek help immediately.

- When narratives alone do not resolve the past, other
techniques, such as Eye Movement Desensitization and
Reprocessing (EMDR), may be added by a professional to
work through trauma issues (see Appendix A).

Bill and Karen sought the assistance of a therapist to help Robert
process through his past losses and traumatic life events. Bill and
Karen chose a baby brontosaurus as the protagonist of their
trauma narrative. Robert has been fascinated with dinosaurs and
repeatedly asks to watch an animated dinosaur video. They
recently took him to a science museum to view a dinosaur exhibit
and he talked about it for days. Robert was relieved to hear that the
story was going to be different today and that he wouldn't have to
listen to that "baby stuff." He sat between his parents as they
began the story. "Once upon a time there was a little tiny dinosaur
inside his egg waiting to be born. But this little egg had a mother
who was just a teenage brontosaurus. She didn't know anything
about taking care of eggs. She just wanted to hang out down at the
big water with her friends. Sometimes she left the egg alone, cold
and unprotected. The baby brontosaurus wasn't growing as fast
and as big as he should have. The big day came and with a loud
crack he came into the world; he was alone. His mother came
along later and showed him where the big water was. He drank
thirstily but his stomach hurt and he didn't know what dinosaurs
should eat. He followed his mother and her friends but they didn't
even look at him and he had to move fast to avoid being trampled
on. Sometimes they shoved him with their great feet if he was in the

way. One day he fell and got a big cut on the back of his head. He found things to eat but sometimes it hurt his stomach bad. Nobody paid him much attention or told him what was good to eat and what would make him sick." Robert moved, talked, and seemed distracted as usual. Bill and Karen were by now sure he was hearing every word and continued the story until the baby found a safe herd who would teach him and care for him.

In the second session with the therapist, Robert wouldn't sit still. He wandered around the room touching things as Bill and Karen told another dinosaur story. They added more detail and began to describe the inner thoughts and feelings of the baby dinosaur. Although he looked disinterested, he made comments that the baby was sad or mad or that the mother wasn't "nice."

Bill and Karen told versions of this story at home between sessions with the therapist. When Robert began to seem bored with the narrative, they told a new trauma narrative, this time with a human protagonist. Robert was getting used to story time and didn't argue about sitting between them and even sat on Karen's lap sometimes. "Once upon a time," Karen began, "there was a girl named Tiffany. Tiffany lived with her mom. Her mom said her dad had left before she was born. Tiffany was 15. Her mom sometimes had boyfriends stay overnight and they would do mean things to Tiffany. So one day Tiffany ran away. She drank alcohol and used drugs with her friends. She didn't care about going to school. She just liked to have fun with her friends. One day she found out she was pregnant. That means there was a baby growing inside her. Tiffany was only 15, just a teenager. She wasn't ready to be a mother. She still drank and used drugs and had fun with her friends. That wasn't good for the baby inside her. She didn't go to the doctor either to make sure her baby was healthy. When the baby was born she knew she would have to go home. The street isn't a place for babies. She named her baby boy Rory. Tiffany didn't know much about babies. She tried to take care of him when he cried, she really did. But no one taught her how to make bottles or give her baby a bath. And when Rory cried and cried, her mother and the boyfriend would yell at her. Sometimes she just left and went to find her friends. Rory would cry and rub his cheek on the bed until he fell asleep. He was hungry and mad and scared. It wasn't Rory's fault his mom left. Babies don't know how to talk. They only know how to cry. Rory deserved to be picked up and loved and fed and rocked and played with. But Tiffany just didn't know how to be a mommy." In Karen's lap, Robert sat very still. He seemed to be listening intently with a very serious look on his face. Karen and Bill kept going until Rory was safe in a new home with new parents. They tried to give voice to what they thought was going on inside Robert. Rory didn't like being told "no" because he had always been his own boss in his first family. And how Rory got into lots of trouble, not because he was a bad kid but because he didn't know how to be part of a family yet. They emphasized how much Rory was learning as he grew up into a big boy.

Problem-solving tips

Trauma narratives are difficult for both parents and children. Hearing the child's past history may be painful and sad; however, empathy for the child may increase. Telling the story replaces chaotic memories and feelings with a coherent narrative, helping the child make sense of the past. Children often form new conclusions about the events. Some children may resist. "Not that story again!" It is important to consider the meaning of the resistance. Commonly asked questions are answered below.

My child refuses to listen to the stories any more. I still think there is more of his history to process. What can I do to engage him?

Finding out why the child is refusing to listen can help determine how to approach this problem. Refusal or apparent boredom may indicate that the child is done with this story, at least for the time being. Other children may be indicating, by refusing to listen to the trauma narrative, that they are having difficulty coping with it. They may need a break or perhaps need additional coping skills to continue. The story's character can model for the child how to deal with difficult emotions, thoughts, and even dreams that may arise during and after the narratives.

Some children are fearful that they might get into trouble for what happened. They might fear that their birth parent or someone else they care about would be in trouble. Many abused children have been threatened. They are fearful that they will be found and punished for telling. If the child is anxious, returning to claiming narratives may reassure him that he deserved responsive care and love. The character in the narrative can also experience the same fear but courageously learn to face the fear.

She may come to realize it wasn't her fault and that her new parents will keep her safe.

If you assess that the child is resisting for some other reason, construct a narrative that addresses the underlying cause of the refusal. One mother noted that her daughter was complaining about hearing the "boring billy goat story" all the time, so she changed the cast of characters and began revealing more details of the trauma history. During the new narrative the girl called out to her birth sibling, "Joey, now we're bears!"

Now that her story is out in the open, my daughter brings it up at inappropriate times. Should I let her talk about it? I'm afraid if I set a limit she'll stop talking

In many cases, children are reluctant to share information about the past. However, others have poor boundaries. They reveal disturbing details about their trauma histories to teachers, friends, or even strangers. Again, determining the underlying reason for the behavior is the first step in addressing this issue. Children with poor boundaries usually need simple rules and lessons communicated through narratives about what most kids talk about in public. Children who use stories about the past to shock and control adults or be the center of attention may respond to narratives addressing the feeling underlying those needs.

We have told the story many times now but she doesn't seem to feel anything. Shouldn't she be mad or sad?

Dissociation allows the child to physically remain with an abusive parent who she depends on for survival. In essence, the child sets aside feelings of hurt, sadness, shame, and anger in order to maintain her relationship with the caregiver. When dissociation is successful the child is able to endure repeated abuse and function in the family, school, and community. During Family Attachment Narrative Therapy children frequently recall past memories of abuse; however, they may not experience the expected emotions during the narrative. Attributing the pain and emotions to the main character may help the child claim, experience, and express her own feelings. Other children appear not to have any feelings about past events or, for that matter, present events that the parent would expect them to be upset about. However, after processing the trauma they are able to feel and express a wider variety of genuine emotions.

My child wiggles and squirms and it's very uncomfortable for me. How do I make her sit still?

It is important to determine the reason that the child is wiggling so the underlying feelings and meaning of the behavior can be addressed in narratives. Increased anxiety expressed through restlessness and fidgeting is normal during trauma narratives and may be calmed when the parent reassures the child of his or her constant and unconditional care and acceptance. Additional tellings of the trauma narrative may desensitize fears brought up by the subject matter. If the child is attempting to push the parent away with the behavior, it may be appropriate to let her know that it is not all right to hurt anyone. Emphasize that story times are important. Vary the story somewhat if the child is bored; change the character or setting. Sometimes telling an adventurous, fun tale that does not have any underlying message keeps the child engaged in the daily storytelling routine.

Some children with attachment issues or past trauma may have a concurrent diagnosis of attention deficit hyperactivity disorder (ADHD). Sitting still is difficult for those children. Allowing them to shift and move during the narratives is fine and does not decrease the effectiveness of the story. For the child with ADHD, moving is a way of maintaining an attentive state. Provide an acceptable means for the child to stay alert. For example, let the child manipulate a soft, squishy ball, or cuddle with a favorite toy. A short break with a drink or snack may help the child continue to pay attention. Some children will move about the room during the story, yet are listening closely.

Summary

Trauma narratives provide a means for the child to process the events, thoughts, and feelings of her early life experiences. The love and comfort the child receives in the safety of her parent's arms communicates that she did not deserve what happened and that it is not her fault. As in claiming narratives, parental attunement to the child guides the selection of characters, the content, the intensity of emotions, and length of the story. Discovering the unique meaning of resistance and difficult behaviors during and following the narratives leads to adjustments in the narrative process. The experience of parental attunement and unconditional acceptance makes the old inner working model obsolete. Trauma narratives decrease the anger, hurt, shame, and sadness associated with the traumatic memory and allows the child to form a new meaning for her experiences.

Chapter 6

Developmental Narratives

One saw your first sweet smile, the other dried your tears.

The joy of watching an infant master developmental tasks and pass through stages such as playing peek-a-boo, speaking his first word, taking his first drink from a cup, learning to walk, or doing something "all by myself" contributes to the development of a reciprocal relationship between parent and child. Milestones and other firsts that parents excitedly videotape or record in baby books may be unknown by adoptive parents. Developmental narratives provide parents with an emotional experience of these events. Stories about babies, one-year-olds, two-year-olds, etc. allow parents to experience their older child as an infant or toddler and encourage him to grow and achieve the normal milestones. These narratives provide children with the experience of a caregiver celebrating their accomplishments and reveling in their uniqueness. These shared experiences and the positive feelings aroused by them build the bonds between the parent and child.

Section 1: The Purpose of Developmental Narratives

Trauma or other developmental injuries may impair how a child thinks, interacts with others, and solves problems (Cozolino 2002). He may appear "stuck" emotionally and/or behaviorally at an earlier stage of development. Parents can often accurately assess at what level their child is functioning. For example, they may report that with peers their ten-year-old acts more like a preschooler, dictating what his friends do, rather than negotiating with them. Children deprived of parental encouragement and support may have delays in physical growth, gross and fine motor skills, speech, cognitive, social, and emotional development. A complete discussion of child development is beyond the scope of this book and parents may need to consult other resources in order to construct appropriate developmental narratives. For our purposes, we will focus on areas in which we commonly see altered development in children with an insecure attachment.

Facilitating cognitive development

Lack of attention and care may impede cognitive development. These changes may not be evident until the child grows older and the discrepancy between adaptive age and chronological age increases. Maladaption in the ability of the child to think, solve problems, and play is common.

Sensitive, attuned care conveys to the child that their actions and cues are effective and valued. Deficits in cause and effect thinking may arise when cues are repeatedly ignored or misread by parents. A child whose cries were not answered may not grasp that actions have reactions. Later, he may display the same behavior day after day despite receiving consistent consequences from parents, never seeming to learn from his mistakes. A child who lacks cause and effect thinking may also be a risk taker – constantly putting himself in dangerous situations without the normal fear inhibitions.

Older children who have been deprived of optimal care may remain in the cognitive stage of preoperational thinking or concrete operations. Children view themselves as the center of the world and are very egocentric in the preoperational stage (Piaget and Inhelder 1969). They frequently have difficulty with attribution. For example, if Mom and Dad announce that they are getting a divorce shortly after the child has thrown a tantrum, he may believe that it is his fault. Children in the stage of concrete operations are black and white thinkers, unable to imagine possibilities or see options. Jokes, sarcasm, and witticisms are simply not understood. One 12-year-old who had a background of serious neglect was told by a peer to stop "pulling my leg." She replied in all seriousness, "Mom, I didn't touch her leg." Solving problems is also very difficult for such children. They get stuck repeating the same strategy over and over again even when it seems clear that it will not work. Whining for help and eventually breaking down into tears, a ten-year-old collapsed in frustration after trying over and over to pull a large object through a much smaller opening. She was unable to step back and consider the options of going around the obstacle or removing it.

Delays may also be seen in the play of children who experienced neglect and inadequate stimulation as an infant and toddler. For example, symbolic functioning normally is evidenced between the ages of three to five. In symbolic play children are able to use objects and language to represent something else. The child pretends that a box is a crib or says, "Let's pretend we're at McDonald's." Older children who have a history of trauma and attachment disruption may not demonstrate developmentally appropriate imaginative play with a coherent narrative, but simply manipulate or stack toys like an 18-month-old child. Another example of delayed play is a ten-year-old child who opened and closed the blinds of the therapist's office, playing peek-a-boo with his mother's car.

Before children can use symbols they must master object permanence, or the understanding that objects or people still exist when out of sight. Children normally master this task between the ages of 4 months and 18 months. This ability may be impaired in children who experienced deprivation in their early years. A six-year-old who had been institutionalized for the first three years of life was distressed when told to put a piece of candy in his pocket for later, crying, "But I can't see it!" For him, the candy placed out of sight meant that it had disappeared. Because of his early history, he could not form a mental representation of the candy and know that it was safe in the pocket of his jeans.

Developmental narratives can be used to assist children in moving forward, learning and becoming proficient in areas where they may be lagging behind their peers. Embarrassed and fearing failure, many children may be reluctant to back up and try something they may feel is "babyish." Through imagination and stories children are able to practice these new skills.

Facilitating emotional development

Emotional growth may also be arrested and the child may lack the ability to modulate strong emotions. An infant's ability to accept comfort and eventually develop self-soothing strategies begins to form when a mother, attuned to his cues, relieves the stress and calms the child. A neglected or abused child who has not mastered the ability to accept external comfort or internally soothe himself may be overwhelmed by strong feelings and regress to more primitive coping strategies. Imagine a boy waiting in line, anticipating recess. It's noisy and he's being bumped. This anxiety and stimulation initiates his stress response. Without a pattern to soothe and calm himself, he becomes more agitated and finally strikes out at another child who inadvertently bumped him again. Sitting in the principal's office during recess is unlikely to change this child's internal reaction to stress or his behavior next time he is bumped while waiting in line.

Developmental narratives promote the growth and maturation of patterns that can help the child deal with strong emotions. Physiologically, many emotions may feel similar and may trigger the child's stress response. Learning to tell the difference between excitement and anxiety, or embarrassment and anger, and then expressing those feelings appropriately, can be taught and modeled through narratives.

Building relationships

Socially, children who have been deprived of physical and emotional nurturing lag years behind their peers. They have difficulty recognizing nonverbal cues and misinterpret facial expressions and verbal information. Their attempts to interact are immature and even bizarre. Institutionalized children often display the most severe deficits in peer relationships. Behavior that may have been prevalent and even tolerated in an orphanage may ostracize children in current social situations.

Sasha spent three years in an Eastern European institution before she was adopted. Her sometimes bizarre and intrusive behavior emerged when she entered kindergarten. In a large room filled with lots of children and one adult, she began running around, making odd noises, grabbing others' belongings, bumping into and hitting other children. Although unusual, her behavior made sense in the context of her institutional background. Part of the daily regimen included "play time" when the children were put in a small room with few toys and no supervision.

A Romanian adoptee recalled being in a room full of cribs and silent infants. When asked where she was in that room she replied, "Oh, I'm crying and they're rocking me." She survived by acting in a way that caused the adults around her to pay attention to her. She also learned to be rude to her peers, who she perceived as competition. This attention-getting behavior did not go over well with her new family or with peers in the school setting. New behaviors can be shaped through developmental narratives. Children also learn how to read nonverbal signals as the parent tells stories with emotion and animation.

Disinhibited behavior with adults is common among children who have been neglected. Without an attachment to a primary caregiver, the normal inhibitions about strangers may not develop. Any adult becomes a possible source of attention, food, or gifts. Parents commonly report that their children will approach strangers, hug, sit on their laps, or request help in the bathroom from them. One parent related the chaos her two adopted boys caused in the airport by taking food and belongings from everyone. After using claiming narratives to establish parents' claim to children, developmental narratives may be used to present information about how children behave when they are attached. They learn to prefer the primary attachment figure, check in with them, and exhibit anxiety when separated or when they see a stranger. Narratives can be used to teach caution with strangers and to reinforce that parents are capable of meeting children's needs.

Remedial skill building

Children's maladaptive behavior in a family makes bonding with them more difficult. Lying is frequently a problem in children with attachment disturbances. A tall tale may be cute when coming from the mouth of a three-year-old, when developmentally the line between reality and fantasy is blurred. But the same imaginative tale from a ten-year-old is frustrating to parents. Tantrums with flailing arms and legs accompanied by tears and wailing may be tolerated in preschool. However, teachers in middle school cannot stop everything to soothe and calm an out of control pre-adolescent who was denied extra time on the computer. Daily phone calls from frustrated teachers are often followed by angry confrontations that evening between parents and children. When behavior is viewed as a component of the child's past and a result of disturbed development, the focus is not on a consequence but on "How can we help this 12-year-old learn what he needs to know to survive middle school?" Narratives can teach children the difference between truth and a lie, how to delay gratification, and handle frustration.

Children tend to have periods of regression when mastering a new skill. Learning new behavior is stressful for children. When teaching new skills through narratives, parents can provide permission to regress. One parent allowed her daughter to play daily with baby toys during their nightly bath ritual. Another intuitively knew that on some days her adolescent son was not going to be able to make it through the weekly shopping trip without having a toddler meltdown. She allowed him to stay home with a sitter. When staying home or changing the routine to allow for regression isn't feasible, the parents could tell a story about a child's frustration while learning to do something new. This narrative demonstrates their empathy and attunement to just how hard it is to grow up.

Sasha had a history of early deprivation and delayed development. Her parents discovered that she needs periods when she is allowed to regress. When she just can't hold it together any more, she tells her Mom that she needs to be two, and that being five is too hard. Her mother gives her permission to regress. She stays home from school and experiences all the structure and nurturing necessary for a two-year-old. With her needs met, she can often return to age-appropriate behavior within hours.

Enhancing development

Narratives are an effective tool to encourage growth in children that behave in ways reminiscent of a younger child. What appears to be maladaptive behavior in a ten-year-old may be normal (maybe even cute) for a four-year-old. Seeing the ten-year-old's problem behavior as typical for a four-year-old also provides clues about the child's inner working model and brings up the question of what was happening in the child's life at the time that may have changed his developmental pathway. Parents can then empathize with their child's developmental challenges rather than be angry at the behavior. When observing difficult behavior, parents can ask themselves at what developmental stage or age this behavior would be appropriate and then modify their response to the behavior accordingly. Recognizing the child's need to regress may mean changing parenting techniques. For example, parents respond to stealing in a three-year-old differently than a 13-year-old. Developmental narratives put behaviors in context of developmental needs and stages. When behavior is seen as consistent with the child's inner working model and as normal for his stage of development, it no longer appears pathological. When the behavior is identified in this way parents enjoy watching and being the child's cheerleader as he moves ahead.

Putting difficult behaviors in the context of altered developmental pathways not only changes the way parents discipline their children but also decreases the shame children may experience about their behavior.

Labeling behavior from a developmental perspective gives children feedback on their behavior and defines goals and privileges to work toward. Two-year-olds who whine and have tantrums don't get to stay up until nine o'clock watching movies like ten-year-olds. When children hear the privileges available to older children they may strive to act their age.

> Sasha's parents successfully drew a distinction between orphanage behavior and "family" behavior using stories about an adopted animal. Wanting to be like the story's character, she eagerly practiced her new "family" behaviors both at school and home. Sasha was able to label her own behavior, proudly calling herself a "family girl."

Summary

Children who have been traumatized in the early years of life may behave like a much younger child. There are physical, cognitive, emotional, and social delays. Cognitive concepts such as object permanence, causality, and symbolic function may not appear until much later than expected. Emotionally, the child may have difficulty modulating feelings and become overwhelmed. Children who are raised in chaotic environments may not recognize social cues and respond inappropriately to their peers. These delays are not permanent. In a safe, consistent, supportive environment, the child is free to move ahead cognitively and emotionally. Physical and neurological growth can be re-mediated. In fact, studies have shown that children adopted from institutions grow at a very fast rate once they are in a nurturing environment (Johnson 2004). Attuned parents can create new patterns for responses to stress. Developmental narratives teach children how to grow up. Cognitive, emotional, and social skills improve when parents lovingly encourage and support children as they struggle to master new tasks.

Section 2: Telling Developmental Narratives

Developmental narratives encourage children to move through developmental stages that they missed when they were simply surviving in an abusive, neglectful environment. We have found that many traumatized or deprived children want to behave better at home. They want to have friends, but just don't know how. They don't have the necessary skills to succeed in family and social situations. Hearing stories about what they would have been like at an earlier developmental stage teaches children what is "normal." Developmental narratives educate both parents and children about a range of behaviors that children typically present at various stages of growth. Both may recognize stages and behaviors that were missed. Parents can then encourage children as they struggle to move forward. Older children are able to evaluate and label their own behavior. Following narratives it is common to hear a child state, "I'm really being eight, aren't I, Mom?" Children and their new parents engage in stories, play, or re-enactments, which allow them both to experience the pride of mastering developmental tasks.

> After telling developmental narratives to her daughter, one very surprised parent related the following story. Expecting an immediate meltdown when she said "no" to a cookie, she waited and it did not happen. Her daughter paused as if thinking. "But I really want a cookie," she said. Mom empathetically and firmly said no again. Once more she waited, expecting the scream. Nothing happened. Her daughter paused again and then just groaned with a disappointed, frustrated tone in her voice. No meltdown. The parent could not believe it. Later, her daughter talked about the incident and said that she had been thinking hard about whether she should get mad like a two-year-old or act like a six-year-old. She wasn't exactly sure what a six-year-old would do so she groaned. "Was that OK, Mom?" After daily tantrums for the past four years, it was definitely OK with Mom.

When you were a two-year-old you would have...

Developmental narratives begin at an age where the child missed some critical emotional or physical nurturing or experienced a traumatic life event. For some, this may have occurred in the prenatal stage and the developmental narrative should begin at the point of conception.

> Once upon a time there was a mommy and daddy whale who lived in a deep blue ocean called the Pacific. This mommy and daddy decided that they wanted to have a baby whale to swim and play with them. They traveled south to the warm waters, where they spent the winter waiting for the baby to be born. The mommy and

daddy whale loved the baby whale before he was even born. The mommy ate lots of plankton to make sure her baby would grow big and strong inside her. She stayed away from the poisons they sometimes found in the water because she knew that the poison would hurt her baby. The daddy swam close to protect the mother from hunters…

Even if the child's complete history is not known, his current behavior may give clues to the emotional and physical care that may have been lacking. A child who refuses to dress himself may be perceived as oppositional or as expressing a desire to be nurtured. A child who hugs strangers and will sit on anyone's lap may not have mastered the primary developmental task of attachment. When analyzing behavior, continually ask what the child might be thinking or feeling. What is the meaning of the behavior? Is this behavior related to the child's early attachment experience or past trauma that may have caused him to miss a key developmental task or stage, to take a maladaptive pathway?

Jenny's foster parents knew that she had been passed around between relatives and friends and neighbors. Her parents were addicted to crack cocaine and had been in and out of jail. Jenny had been born while her birth mother was incarcerated. She spent her first month of life with her grandmother. When her mother got out she found her dealer before she found her daughter. She would leave Jenny with a babysitter and not come back for days. At four Jenny treated all adults the same. She hugged everyone. She ran off in the department store and her foster mom would find her chatting happily to another customer. It got so bad that as soon as she heard the loudspeaker, she knew it would be an announcement for "Jenny's mom to meet her at the customer service desk." Her foster parents were scared for her. Her disinhibition made her vulnerable. They had talked until they were blue in the face about stranger danger but she didn't heed their warnings. Mom and Dad decided to try a story about how babies learn who their parents are and don't like strangers. One Sunday morning as they were all snuggled together on their big kingsize bed, Mom said, "Jenny, we have a story we would like to tell instead of reading the comics today, OK?"

"OK," Jenny chirped happily. "Once upon a time there was a new mommy and daddy. Their baby had just been born. When babies are born they are wide awake for a while so the mom and dad held him close. The new baby looked around until he came to his mother's face. He stopped. His eyes stared into her eyes almost like he was trying to memorize her face. He looked at her for a long time, then he looked away. Pretty soon his eyes found their way back to hers and they gazed at each other for a good long time. Eventually he fell asleep. But he never forgot those eyes. They were the first things he looked for when he woke up."

"What was the baby's name?" Jenny asked.

"The mommy and daddy named him Charlie because that was his grandpa's name. Charlie spent most days sleeping, eating, and growing. But each time his mommy or daddy fed him, they held him close and they stared into each other's eyes. As he got old enough to play, he would reach up his chubby little fist and touch his daddy's beard or grab his mommy's glasses. They played pat-a-cake and this little piggy. He would watch them with big eyes, smiling and drooling and blowing spit bubbles."

"Spit bubbles! That's funny!" exclaimed Jenny.

"That's just what babies do," Dad said.

"Pretty soon little Charlie was sitting up. He watched his mommy vacuum or do the dishes. Sometimes he would shake his rattle and then look to see if his mommy was watching. She was always there smiling, clapping her hands and saying, 'What a big boy Charlie.' After a couple more months Charlie started crawling around. He could chase after the cat or explore the den. But he never went very far from his mommy. Charlie followed her from room to room and if he couldn't find her he'd start to cry."

"Why did he cry?" Jenny asked.

"Charlie could not see his mommy; he got scared," Mom replied.

"I don't get scared when you get lost," Jenny proudly asserted.

"I know," said Dad with a wry grin. "But maybe if you had been with us from the very beginning you would have learned that it was safe to stick close to Mom and Dad."

Mom continued, "Remember how Charlie memorized his mommy and daddy's face? Well at about the same time that he started crawling, he started to be afraid of faces he didn't know. If someone walked up to the stroller and said, 'Oh what a cute baby!' he'd cry and look for his mommy and daddy. He cried because he didn't know who that person was. Babies go through a stage when they are afraid of strangers. They only want their mommies and daddies to take care of them. Charlie would sometimes cry if Grandma and Grandpa held him."

"That's silly, he should know his grandma and grandpa," said Jenny.

"Charlie did know his grandma and grandpa," Mom explained. "But if he could see his mommy, that's who he wanted. Charlie kept getting bigger and soon he was walking. He could toddle off toward the swings at the park all by himself now. He kept looking back at his daddy, just to make sure he was watching. He was big enough to stay in the nursery at church now. He cried when mommy and daddy left and watched them go all the way down the hall. Eventually he stopped crying and would play a little. When they came back, he smiled a great big smile. He put his arms up high so they would pick him up. At home he could play by himself for a little while. He didn't follow mommy around any more but she talked to him as she moved around the house cleaning so he always knew where she was. Sometimes he would go find her and show her a toy. One day they went to the department store. He didn't want to ride in the cart; he wanted to walk. So Mommy showed him how to hang on to the side of the cart so he wouldn't get lost. At the checkout lane, the nice lady asked him if he wanted a piece of candy. He hid behind his mommy's leg and wouldn't even look at her. Mommy had to take the candy for him."

"Not me! I would have taken the candy!" interjected Jenny.

"Charlie knew his mommy and daddy were safe; he didn't trust strangers," said Mom. "It's a mom and dad's job to teach their children not to trust strangers. Maybe if you had been with us from the first, you would have learned that moms and dads are safe and that strangers could be dangerous."

"Oh," said Jenny.

"What do you say we go make some french toast?" asked Dad.

"OK!" said Mom and Jenny in unison.

The hero of the story can be the child, a favorite animal, story, or cartoon character. When the protagonist of the story is a character that the child identifies with, the hero's challenge becomes the child's challenge. The child then can take on the attitude and perspective of the character. In the telling, the main character experiences the love and care necessary to support mastery of developmental tasks appropriate to the stage that is the focus of the story. The length of the story depends on the age and attention span of the child. A young child listening to the normal development and behavior of a one-, two-, or three-year-old may feel overwhelmed with expectations and information. Stories are more effective if they focus on one developmental task, stage, or age rather than multiple stages. For example, one parent constructed a story focused on the concept of object permanence. The story was about a little girl who lived in an orphanage and was adopted by a family in the United States. In the orphanage caregivers, toys, and other belongings were not constant. They changed continuously and disappeared. In her new family, the little girl learned that mommies always come back and that toys stay where they are left.

The plot of developmental narratives typically focuses on a particular task or stage the child has not yet mastered. Emphasize the protagonist's desire to grow and accomplish the task. The hero doesn't have to succeed immediately; he can struggle, overcome, and experience regressions just as the child hearing the narrative. Describe the character's efforts, persistence, and attitude while accomplishing the task. Not all experiences in life have happy endings; neither should every story. Although narratives encourage new behaviors and mastery of tasks, failures and setbacks are a real part of a child's experience of growing up, so include them as well.

As mentioned previously, props and re-enactments may help the child understand and assimilate the information. Filming a ten-year-old taking tentative steps between his mom and dad may initially seem silly, but it may fill a longing for a child who has no pictures from his early childhood. We have watched a seven-year-old struggle like a two-year-old to fit shapes into the right hole and a five-year-old lie on a baby quilt contentedly playing with baby rattles. Children seem to understand that they missed something back then, something that they need to go back to and experience. There are no limits; be creative and have fun with the narratives.

"If you had been our one-year-old back then, we would have been there to cheer and clap when you took your very first step. Daddy would have had the video camera out ready to go all the time so we would not have missed that exciting moment. You had already started pulling yourself up on furniture. You would have walked from one end of the couch to the other. But one special day you would have turned, let go, and taken your first step. We would have been right there with our arms reaching out to encourage you and catch you if you wobbled."

Five-year-old Nate fell on his bottom right on cue and laughed with his adoptive parents. Suddenly, a little embarrassed, Nate said, "This is stupid, I'm not a baby."

"No you're not, but we didn't get to take pictures of your first steps. You were in Romania; we were still in America waiting for you," said Mom. "Let's go get some frozen yogurt; babies and big boys eat that, don't they?"

Bill and Karen speculated that Robert was functioning in the range of an 18- to 24-month-old child. He had an intense drive to get what he wanted and do things independently. In their minds they could visualize him as a toddler struggling to reach the cupboard where the crackers are kept. He still tries over and over again to do things by himself and then collapses in frustration when his efforts are thwarted. Robert refuses assistance, attempts to distract him, and any reassurance and comfort. They admire his persistence. Bill and Karen also recognize that four-year-old Robert is much smarter than an 18-month-old. He has learned many more strategies to get into that cupboard. Robert's level of functioning was assessed using a Vineland Adaptive Behavior Scale. The detailed parent interview confirmed that Robert was indeed operating much more like a toddler than a preschooler in day-to-day activities. They noted that his receptive communication, interpersonal relationship, and coping skills were delayed. Could it be that some of his oppositional behavior was in fact a lack of understanding of what was being asked of him? Could his aggression in preschool be caused by not knowing how to approach peers, share during activities, or use words when frustrated?

At home, Bill and Karen began to simplify their communication and directions when talking with Robert. They gave one-step instructions, paired directions with visual cues, and demonstrated tasks for him. It didn't solve all their problems but he was a little less defiant. Bill and Karen decided to focus on teaching Robert how to share utilizing developmental narratives. They initially decided to use the same baby brontosaurus as the protagonist in this story.

"This story is about the baby dinosaur again," started Karen.

"Not again," groaned Robert.

"Well, who should the story be about today?" asked Karen, sidestepping a possible argument by recognizing Robert's cue and changing the protagonist.

"I want a story about elephants!"

"OK, George the baby elephant had trouble making friends in the herd. He tried to get the other baby elephants to play with him. He would bump them, tease them, and sometimes he would grab something away from them hoping that they would chase him, but they never did. But when an elephant tried to play with George, George would nudge all his toys into a pile with his long trunk and stand over them. He didn't want anyone to take them away. So the elephant would walk away and go play with someone else that had toys. George was mad. George was sad too. George wasn't being bad or mean [words Robert had probably heard to describe him], he just didn't know how to play with friends. None of the adults in the herd had taught him. One day a wise old elephant stood rubbing her tough skin against a tree. She saw that all the other baby elephants stayed away from George. She saw him guarding his toys but not really having any fun with them. She had been around so long that she knew every elephant in the herd. Her name was Jumbo."

"Oh, just like Dumbo's mom," said Robert.

"Yes, just like Dumbo's mom. Jumbo remembered that this baby elephant's mom was just a young elephant. She had a baby before she knew how to take care of babies. Jumbo decided that she would adopt this baby elephant and teach him everything he needed to know to be in a herd. The next time another elephant came to play with George's toys, she was right there and told him to push a toy closer to his new friend. 'Watch what the other elephant does with the toy, George. And then you take a turn and do exactly what he is doing.' George tried it and the elephant didn't leave. They took turns playing for a long time and then the other baby elephant had to go home to sleep. George wasn't sad that night." Bill and Karen constructed a developmental narrative to teach Robert the basics of "how to be a friend." Unlike other times when they had tried to coach him through social situations, he didn't get defensive and respond with "I know that already!" He seemed amused by the baby elephant's poor attempts at making friends and even told them what the elephant should do next time. Each time Robert faced a new social situation, Bill and Karen were able to use the baby elephant to model behavior for Robert.

Problem-solving tips

Developmental narratives encourage progress toward more age-appropriate behavior. Commonly asked questions are answered below.

What if my child wants to stay a baby?

Once a child's emotional and physical needs are met, he is able to move forward developmentally. If a child wants to listen to the infant stories over and over again, there is most likely a reason, some need that he is attempting to satisfy. New narratives may be introduced, telling the child what he would have been like as a one-, two-, three-, or four-year-old while the parent allows periods within each day for the child to hear or re-enact the infancy stage. The child may move back and forth between ages and stages until the developmental needs are met. The feeling of safety and security does not happen overnight. Everyday stresses may cause the child to regress at times; but there is a drive toward growth, so don't give up.

This is my first child and I adopted him when he was seven. I don't know what infants and younger children do

Before constructing a developmental narrative, new parents or parents of older children may need to review basic child development books such as: *The First Twelve Months of Life* (Caplan 1973), *The First Three Years of Life* (White 1975), and the classic *The Common Sense Book of Baby and Child Care* (Spock 1945). Social workers, therapists, and other professionals may also be able to assist parents. Children may identify with the narrative if they recall how younger siblings, or infants and toddlers observed in the extended family, church, or neighborhood, behaved at the age the narrative is taking place.

My son is stuck in the "terrible twos." How do I get him to move forward fast?

When a child is behaving like a two-year-old, it may be tempting to start developmental narratives at age three in an attempt to grow him up quickly through the terrible twos. A focus on the need behind the behavior is critical. A child will only move forward developmentally when his basic psychological and emotional needs are met. Determining what is underneath the difficult behavior may cue parents where to begin a developmental narrative.

Summary

Developmental narratives help children master the "how to's" of childhood while providing parents with the emotional experience of parenting a child through earlier stages of development. Cognitive, emotional, and social deficits may be ameliorated as children progress through ages, stages, and phases by identifying with the narrative's hero. Understanding that children are functioning at a much lower adaptive level than might be expected given their chronological age decreases confrontation and anger in the family. This perspective helps parents view difficult behavior as a need for knowledge and skills. Armed with the knowledge that children need their help, parents teach and cheer them on. Adversaries become teammates working toward the same goals. This shift in how parents view behavior is a critical factor in improving the emotional connection between parents and children.

Chapter 7

Successful Child Narratives

One gave you a talent, the other gave you aim.

A child who has been hurt in the past may behave in ways that drive parents crazy. Many challenging behaviors develop in order to help the child survive physically and emotionally in a neglectful, abusive environment and can be difficult to change. Some problem behaviors occur simply because the child lacks the basic skills of how to do life. Overwhelming emotions such as fear, anxiety, sadness, or anger instigate other behaviors.

The majority of parents contact our clinic because the child has extremely difficult behaviors. They have read book after book, attended workshops, sought the help of educators and professionals, and still the child has defeated every parenting strategy. They feel angry, frustrated, and defeated. Behaviors exhibited by a child with attachment issues go far beyond the bounds of developmentally normal problem behaviors. The narratives used in Family Attachment Narrative Therapy help children create new stories about who they are, what happened to them, and who they can be. New stories teach and guide new behavior (Cozolino 2002). Successful child narratives address the child's behavior problems, giving the parents the relief they seek.

Section 1: The Purpose of Successful Child Narratives

In the telling of successful child narratives, the parent's goal is not to confront the child's behavior but rather to use stories to support and encourage the child as she learns to control whether or not she behaves in a respectful, responsible way. Many problem behaviors can be addressed through enjoyable narratives while teaching the child values, reinforcing cause and effect thinking, presenting alternative behaviors, and explaining the basics of how to do life. Successful child narratives are extremely useful to teach, guide, and direct all children. Use of claiming, trauma, and developmental narratives usually precedes successful child narratives with a child who has an insecure attachment. Attachment provides the support needed as she tries out new behaviors. The experience of attunement with a trustworthy, responsive caregiver is necessary to shift the child's negative inner working model. It is important for parents to be attuned to their child's feelings. Why is the child behaving this way? Successful child narratives are most effective when the underlying feelings and purpose of the behavior are understood.

Teaching children values

Values are best conveyed within the safety and security of an attachment relationship. The interactions between a parent and child involve both verbal and nonverbal communications. In this exchange of information the parent communicates values, ideals, and a way of viewing the world. This is the process of moral development. As the child learns to talk, this process becomes an internal dialogue. The parent's voice is present, guiding and helping the child to judge whether or not an action is acceptable. Small children can sometimes be heard repeating parental prohibitions out loud even as they impulsively disobey a rule. Because of the emotional bond between parents and children, they usually make the right choice to avoid disappointing the parent and causing a rift in the relationship. Many parents of older adopted children report that their children seem to lack the intrinsic motivation to please others or make the right choice. Successful child narratives can be used to convey values, right choices, and ways of behaving.

Reinforcing cause and effect thinking

Cause and effect thinking begins to develop in the first months of life when the child experiences that actions cause reactions. Cries result in nursing and rocking, smiles and coos lead to reciprocal smiles and sounds, throwing a rattle to the floor causes a strange, new sound and then, predictably, Mom or Dad pick it up. When there is a consistent reaction, the infant or toddler begins to realize that she has an impact on others and the world. Conversely, when the infant does not experience predictable, congruent responses to her cues, she may feel powerless and fail to understand that actions have consequences. Successful child narratives contain dilemmas, choices, and consequences to reinforce cause and effect thinking. As the parents respond to the child's cues during the storytelling, the child experiences the power of her actions and feels valued and important.

Presenting alternative behaviors

Children who have been abused or neglected early in life may have cognitive, emotional, and social delays. Their ability to cope with everyday stress and problems is limited. When angry or fearful, they do not see options. Coping strategies that would be appropriate for a toddler or preschooler are used over and over again by much older children unable to conceive of alternatives. Instead they may choose a response that is familiar. They may emulate adults they observed in a previous home or resort to behaviors that appear to lack insight and organization. Because of impaired cause and effect thinking they continue to use the same inadequate tactics to handle problems despite repeated failure. They are unable to evaluate what went wrong or formulate a new plan. Successful child narratives provide alternatives to habitual negative behaviors and increase children's coping abilities. A classic example is a ten-year-old throwing herself to the floor of the grocery store wailing for candy. When a two-year-old does not get her way, she may resort to pouting, whining, and tantrums, which sometimes work. When a ten-year-old behaves like that two-year-old in public, parents may want to pull a hat down over their face and sneak out the back door. Successful child narratives give the child alternatives to her inappropriate behavior. Sometimes a quick story about a greedy, green alien named "I want it" may distract and change the moods of both parent and child. But if the child is lying on the floor screaming at the top of her lungs, doing a story at that moment seems ludicrous and other parenting strategies may come in handy (see Conclusion for parenting resources).

Explaining the basics of how to do life

Problem behaviors may be a way of covering for deficits in social and emotional skills. Children consider their own life experience as "normal" and assume every other family is the same, even if that "normal" included physical, emotional, and sexual abuse. In a new family "normal" might be very different from past experience. New ways of doing things, new routines, new rules, new expectations can be bewildering. Vacations, daycare, shopping, school buses, and many more situations may be novel to adopted children. They lack the basic knowledge of everyday life. Successful child narratives can be used to teach countless ways of behaving in every situation.

Summary

Difficult behavior frequently sends parents looking for help. Trying to change behavior without an emotional bond between the parent and child is frustrating. The child may respond to behavior management plans if the reward is sweet enough or the consequences severe. However, despite careful implementation and consistent follow through, the child does not seem to integrate the new behaviors and returns to the old behavior as soon as the goal is reached. Parents frequently complain that their child lacks any internal motivation to improve. Discovering the meaning of the behavior, how it is related to the child's early attachment and trauma history, and whether it is related to developmental delays is the key to changing problem behaviors in a child with insecure attachment. Successful child narratives support and encourage the child as she struggles to make changes in behavior. A child may be afraid of making a mistake, afraid of asking for help, afraid of accepting love. These narratives can teach values, new behaviors, life logistics, and reinforce cause and effect thinking.

Section 2: Telling Successful Child Narratives

Successful child narratives teach new behaviors to a child who may not have the coping skills to deal with everyday stress and disappointments. The underlying message is that the child's behavior is just behavior and does not define the child. Successful child narratives are most effective when one understands the meaning of the child's behavior. Once the underlying feeling and the meaning of the behavior are determined, those thoughts and feelings can be attributed to the character in the story. Some possible meanings of difficult behaviors are discussed below.

The meaning of behavior

There are many possible reasons or meanings for a child's behavior. Although it may appear that the child is committing premeditated acts of

destruction and defiance, we have often found that the child is responding to past trauma and life experiences or operating from a deficit.
Defiance is safer than admitting that she doesn't know how to do something or doesn't understand what was said to her. Defiance is safer than
accepting help from an adult, or having to feel sad, lonely, hurt, or vulnerable. Difficult behavior is then understood as an attempt to cope with
everyday stress. Some maladaptive behaviors are a result of missing
developmental tasks and stages, or the basics of how to do life, while
concentrating all her energies on surviving. Many behaviors are
designed to express anger and reduce the ever-present feelings of
anxiety and sadness.

Reducing the effects of stress

In an attempt to reduce fear and anxiety many children want to be in
control of everything and everyone. Children who have survived chaotic
and dangerous situations did so by learning to take care of themselves.
Children attempt to get their needs met by acting demanding or by
manipulating adults. Children identified as having a disorganized/dis-
oriented pattern of interacting with parents try to control the parent by
using aggressive, punitive behavior or manipulative caregiving strategies
(Jacobvitz and Hazen 1999; Main and Cassidy 1988). Eating disorders,
pica (eating nonfood items), stealing, and hoarding food may be related
to children's early emotional and physical neglect and deprivation
(Chesney and Spencer 2004). In a new home with their basic physical
and emotional needs taken care of, needs become wants. The perception
that the needs will not be met causes anxiety. Children intensify their
efforts to get what they want until every interaction seems like a negotia-
tion. In their early experiences, being in control meant the difference
between being hurt or making it through another day. Underlying the
need to be in control is fear. As such, it is a very difficult behavior to
modify. The more parents try to control children, the more threatened
they feel and the harder they resist. For the anxious child, control is
soothing balm for her fears.

Stealing and lying may also be the child's attempt at reducing stress.
The traumatized child may attempt to satisfy her needs by stealing.
However, this becomes a more serious problem when a child whose
needs are now being met seeks to get what she wants by taking. In
addition, the higher levels of anxiety felt by the child may lead her to
conceal mistakes and misbehavior. Lying becomes a way to protect

herself. Control may play a role in this behavior; it is as if telling the truth somehow gives the adult power over her.

A child may also attempt to reduce stress by resisting emotional connections with adults. Shallow, phony behavior is designed to keep distance between the child and adults and avoid the discomfort of intimacy and strong emotions. She may approach adults indiscriminately, as if grooming them as future caregivers. Constant talking and questions keep the parent's attention focused on her while deflecting a deeper connection.

Many children with attachment disturbances have well-developed observation skills. They are vigilant and watch everyone and everything. They quickly size up the situation and adults around them. Children may seem to be able to read the mind of others (van der Kolk 1996). They know what to say and what emotions they should be feeling and act the part appropriately. At other times, however, they appear oblivious to those around them and react insensitively to their needs.

Children who have experienced deprivation or abuse may operate in a constant state of alert. They are anxious about everything. Even an event that the parents think will make the child happy may cause stress. In the rush to ready for an out of town trip, tempers flare and stress is abundant. The last thing parents need is children who are whining or disrespectful. It can be the last straw. Defiance as the family is packing for a vacation may be caused by fear of the unknown. Leaving behind the familiar and experiencing something new is an exciting part of most vacations. However, for children with an insecure attachment, it can be terrifying. In addition, packing belongings and loading up the car may remind the child of the many moves he had in the past. Fear of abandonment and loss may result in opposition to the parent's every request. Understandably, such defiance may leave the parent exhausted, exasperated, and ready to haul the bags back into the house.

Developmental needs

Difficult behavior also originates in developmental delays due to the child's history, institutionalization, fetal alcohol syndrome or effects, or other neurological deficits. Defiance may be due to a lack of basic knowledge about how to do life. Many children who do not understand what is being asked of them simply refuse to cooperate. Opposition often results in behavioral consequences rather than remedial teaching of the necessary skills to do what is required of them. Lying may also be related to arrested development. Remember, chronological age does not equal developmental and emotional ages. If the child is stuck in an ego-centric preschool stage she may believe that if she wishes it, it is so, and if she says it, it will be believed.

Impaired social skills are also related to the child's past history. Lack of positive, nurturing, attachment relationships impede the development of social abilities. The child has difficulty interpreting and responding to cues. The child's social behavior may actually be appropriate for her delayed stage of emotional development. Without those predictable interactions, a child may fail to develop the ability to understand cause and effect. Later she acts without considering consequences and has difficulty learning from mistakes. Difficulty with cause and effect also seems to impair conscience development. Without a secure attachment to a primary caregiver the child does not identify with or internalize her parents' values. Because she didn't experience an attuned, responsive caregiver, she in turn has difficulty understanding the thoughts and feelings of others. Children who do not develop empathy do not appear to feel guilt and remorse.

Expressing emotions

The threat of abandonment and loss arouses intense anger. Bowlby (1973, 1988) believed that the goal of this anger is to deter the parent from leaving. When the parent fails to respond appropriately, the child's behavior may become increasingly disorganized and deviant. Children that have a disorganized attachment often exhibit aggressive behaviors (Lyons-Ruth 1996). This anger and aggression may be repressed or directed at other targets (foster parents, siblings, pets, and property) when the child must maintain the relationship with the parent. An unavailable parent or loss of a caregiver may also be associated with depression (Bowlby 1980). Depressed feelings may be expressed in feelings of hopelessness and withdrawal from the family or even self-injurious behaviors and suicidal thoughts and attempts.

Oppositional behavior is also very common and may be a way of expressing anger or the child may simply be emulating or recreating past experiences. Anger and the need for revenge may lead to stealing and destruction of property. Some children with attachment disturbances seem driven to destroy themselves, the family, and belongings. Underneath the anger is sadness, frustration (when he doesn't get what he wants), or fear – emotions that make the child feel vulnerable.

Changing behaviors with narratives

Successful child narratives may provide a role model for behavior change. No child likes to be told that she has done something wrong or be told what to do. Stories about how Joey the Kangaroo sits quietly at his desk and raises his hand to answer questions models respect without causing the child's defense system to go on red alert. The character's behavior is clearly labeled as respectful or not respectful. The behavior is viewed as separate from the character. The character is always valued and loved even though the behavior is not.

As with the other narratives, effective stories involve one or more characters with whom the child might identify. Describe the character and the setting. Where does the action take place? Who else is involved? Explain the dilemma the protagonist encounters, the possible options for solving the problem, the choice the character makes, and the results of the choice. One parent who had a son who refused to do chores told a story about an irresponsible stable boy and the tragic results of his not caring for the horses he loved. The child later said, "I think I'll go home and do my homework." Results may not be that immediate. The child may need to hear the same message several times in order to process the information and gain enough mastery over the skills being presented before she attempts them. A child who has identified with the character often states that she wants to be just like him or her.

Sam didn't like rules. On tough days his mom and dad heard, "I wish I lived with another family!" And they did have a lot of rules. Sam's mom and dad recognized that it must be hard for Sam. Sometimes he saw his friends doing things that he wasn't allowed to do yet. So one night Mom said, "Instead of reading you a story, I want to tell you a story tonight. Once upon a time there was a beaver named Harold. Now everyone knows that beavers are busy. They can't help it; it's just the way they are. Mother Beaver was busy in the beaver home, adding new sticks and more mud, chewing off any sharp ends that might scratch her children, and smoothing the dirt floor with her large, flat tail. Father Beaver was busy in the woods every day, cutting down young sweet trees for his family to eat. He checked his dam across the stream each morning. He carefully examined every branch making sure it was strong and sturdy. Without that dam, his family would be swept away in the fast waters of the stream. But Harold beaver was different. He didn't like to work. Harold was a dreamer. He liked to lie on top of the dam and look for shapes in the clouds. Harold was tired of hearing his mother and father say all day, 'Harold, do this, Harold do that. Harold, Harold, Harold' all day long. He wondered what it would be like not to have parents at all," Mom said.

She did not want the character in the story to say the same thing Sam often did. She figured that if it was too close, he would tune her out. So far so good, so she kept going.

"A world where there was no one telling him what to do. It sounded heavenly. That was his last thought as he drifted off to sleep one warm and sunny afternoon. Harold had the strangest dream that day. He dreamed that when he woke up he was in the beaver home all by himself. But it wasn't his home. At least, he didn't think so. This house had a rough floor and the sticks were slapped together every which way. The mud didn't fill in the holes in the walls and the wind whistled through the cracks. Harold went looking for his mom and dad, but no one was around. He waddled around to the side looking for the tender wood to eat but there was no pile. Well, we all know Harold didn't like to work, so what do you think he did next?" asked Mom.

"Went back to sleep?"

"You got it, Sam, Harold went right back to sleep. But when he woke up later it was still cold and windy and the pile of sweet wood was still missing. So Harold went to play. He went to his favorite meadow and rolled in the soft grass. He climbed the highest hill and watched the clouds and the birds as they flew by. Harold even daydreamed that he was a bird and could fly. It was the best day he could ever remember. Not once had someone told him what to do. He found some branches on the ground; they were dry and hard but he gnawed on them anyway. He made his way back to the house, took a deep long drink of water from the stream, and went to sleep. When he woke in the morning he was hungry and cold. This time he decided he'd better do something about this. He'd better find his parents to tell them that the house needed repair and that they were out of food. He went upstream then downstream. Harold couldn't find them anywhere. Worse, when he went by the dam it was leaking. Water was spilling over the top and through a hole in the middle. He had seen his dad fix holes like that but he had no idea how to do it. Harold remembered his dad saying that if too much water got through, the house might wash away. He sat by the dam for a long time watching. He was getting a little nervous. If he went back to the house, the dam might break and wash him and the house away. Harold couldn't decide what to do. What do you think he decided, Sam?" Mom asked.

"I don't know, his parents are supposed to take care of him," said Sam.

"Well, Harold was one lucky beaver," Mom continued. "The sun went behind a cloud and he woke up. It was all a dream. He ran as fast as beavers can run, which isn't too fast, all the way home. There was his mom smoothing the floor. And the house was warm and cozy against the wind. The pile of sweet wood was right where it was supposed to be. Harold gave his very surprised mom a hug and ran back out the door. He didn't slow down until he found his dad by the dam, which was not leaking. Dad was checking it over carefully anyway. Harold's dad said he was thinking about adding another branch to the top of the dam. It was still spring, he explained, and you could never tell when it might rain. And when Harold's dad asked him if he wanted to help cut one down, what do you think Harold said this time?" asked Mom.

"He said OK?"

"Yep he did. But that doesn't mean that Harold started liking to do his chores. Nope, he never liked doing them. Sometimes he still wished he didn't have parents bossing him around. But by helping with the beaver work, he was learning to take care of himself just like a grown-up beaver."

The protagonist is not perfect. He makes mistakes, poor choices, and has grumpy moods. Some mistakes may be comical; others are tragic. Seeing the consequences of the protagonist's choices improves cause and effect thinking. Using narratives, parents can safely allow the child to experience severe consequences that are the likely result of aggression, stealing, or running away. The stories may provide new alternate ways of solving everyday problems. The child internalizes the new behaviors, adding to her own toolbox of coping strategies.

Parents have used classic storytelling techniques such as suspenseful cliffhangers or letting the child choose the path to keep children interested and involved in story time. Soap opera lovers have tuned in for years to keep abreast of their favorite characters. Each and every Friday the story typically leaves the watcher in suspense and tuning in next time to find out what happens. This can be a very effective technique with children as well. When parents leave the hero in a precarious situation, children look forward to hearing what happens next. When children choose the path, they are given some control over the plot of the story. The protagonist reaches a turning point in the story, a fork in the road literally and figuratively. For example, if he chooses road A, he faces a fire-breathing dragon. If road B is taken, he must cross a raging sea to reach safety. The parallel plots in the story both contain valuable lessons for the hero of the story and for children.

Most children figure out what the story is about and that the character represents them. Children's interest is maintained by varying the story's character, setting, or plot. Children may even resist story time if the intent of every story is changing behavior. A story with no obvious moral message or teaching, such as the favorite character going on a great adventure, may renew their interest. One adolescent immediately recognized that she was the troubled character of her parents' stories. She did not want to listen to any more "stupid" stories. However, she was surprised when her character in a subsequent story was the hero and was helping others solve their problems.

Teaching behavior with narratives

Successful child narratives can also be used to teach the basic skills necessary to get through each day. Stories about taking the school bus, going to church, getting ready in the morning, or personal hygiene provide instruction in areas where the child may be lacking the know how. Repetition of the story allows the child to rehearse these new behaviors in the safety of the relationship with the parent.

Timmy had a problem with remembering. He forgot his homework, he forgot to brush his teeth, he forgot to make his bed. His dad, who had ADD (attention deficit disorder) too, had tried everything he and the professionals could think of to help Timmy. Nothing had worked so far. After consulting with our clinic and learning how to do Family Attachment Narrative Therapy, Dad told the following story. He deliberately exaggerated Webster's forgetfulness. Intuitively he knew that his son felt discouraged that he couldn't remember. Timmy often was heard saying, "I'm stupid." His dad believed that if the story hit too close to home his son would miss the point and hear instead another message that he was "stupid." "There once was a boy named Webster. Every morning when he got up he forgot to change his underwear but he remembered to put pants on when it was cold and shorts when it was warm. He forgot to pack a snack for school but he remembered to eat breakfast. He forgot to shampoo his hair but he remembered to wash behind his ears. He forgot to comb his hair but he remembered to floss his teeth. But every day when he went to the door, his shoes were gone. Webster could never find his shoes. Sometimes one was missing, sometimes both. They were his favorite run-fast shoes. He would look under the sofa, behind the door, on the porch. He'd eventually find them hiding somewhere, but by that time his mom was yelling at him to hurry up and the school bus was outside honking. All the kids would snicker at him when he finally ran to the bus with his shoes in his hands instead of on his feet. When the pretty redhead girl laughed at him, that was the last straw. He had to do something about those shoes! But what? It seemed hopeless. It wasn't his fault his shoes disappeared. Someone must be hiding them! Webster decided to find out who was doing it. So that night after his parents put him to bed, he laid awake waiting. It was hard to stay awake. He talked and sang to himself. He even got up and did jumping jacks. Finally the house fell silent. Webster quietly crept out of bed and made his way down to the back door. His shoes were already gone! His coat was on the floor. There were his hat and mittens over on the table. His backpack and all his papers were on the floor. But no shoes! He couldn't see them anywhere! He was too late. Mom and Dad heard the noise and found him sitting on the rug looking sad. 'What's the matter, Webster? Why are you out of bed?'

'I'm looking for my shoes!' he wailed. 'Someone steals them every night. I thought I could catch them. But I'm too late. They're already gone!'

'We locked all the doors and windows tonight, Webster, just like every night. No one came in to take your shoes.'

'Then where are they?' Dad picked up Webster's backpack. No shoes. He picked up his coat and there was one shoe. He looked under the table and there was the other one. 'Well someone must have moved them,' Webster exclaimed.

'I think we have to do something about the remembering problem,' Mom said gently.

'I remember taking them off,' said Webster.

'Do you remember where you took them off?' asked Mom.

'Noooooo,' admitted Webster.

'Well I think the three of us are pretty smart people. We should be able to figure out how to fix the remembering problem. Anybody got any ideas?' Dad asked.

'Well maybe we could tie Webster's shoes to his feet,' Mom teased.

'Or maybe we could glue them to the floor,' Dad added.

'Or maybe we should paint them red so we can see them,' said Mom. They added silly idea after silly idea until even Webster was smiling again.

'Maybe we should buy ten pairs of the same kind of shoes so we never run out,' said Webster.

'That would cost a lot of money, Webster. You would have to help us pay for all those shoes.'

'Well forget that idea then,' said Webster.

'We could put a special rug right here by the coat hooks,' Mom suggested. 'It could even be red so you couldn't miss it when you came home from school. We could paint a picture of shoes on it or write your name on it so you would remember that it was your shoe rug.'

'I don't know,' said Webster.

'Maybe you should keep your shoes on all the time, even in the shower or in bed. Then they would never get lost,' offered Dad.

'I'm out of ideas,' said Mom. 'Maybe we should think about it and talk again tomorrow. It's getting late and we all have school and work tomorrow.'

'OK,' said Webster, feeling a little bit better."

"So what did Webster do?" asked Timmy.

"I don't know," said Dad. "We'll have to wait until tomorrow to find out."

Parents and professionals may be tempted to add a few "words of wisdom" after the story or to question the child to make sure she got the message. Resist the temptation. After completing a fun and creative story to help her son with his anxiety, one parent asked about what he had thought about the story. He abruptly cut her off saying, "Mom, I got it." They do get it. If the adult initiates discussions about how the child can act just like the character, the child may feel shame and then defensiveness. The end result is a lost teaching opportunity.

Robert's behavior was predictable. Every night he pretended to be asleep. After the house was quiet, he would sneak out of his room and get into everything. He ate the cake Karen had baked for another child's birthday the next day. He colored on papers in Bill's desk. He played with toys that did not belong to him and sometimes destroyed them in the process. Knowing that he was wandering the house while she slept made Karen feel uneasy. Other family members were understandably angry when their stuff was wrecked. Bill and Karen hypothesized that this behavior may have evolved in the birth home. Most likely Robert's early life was chaotic. Parties may have lasted into the early morning hours. There may have been music blaring and bright lights on at all times of the day and night. With no set routine for meals or bedtime, Robert foraged for food when he was hungry and slept wherever and whenever he was tired. This theory helped them to understand the meaning of Robert's nighttime behavior. They now speculated that the behavior might be Robert's way of taking care of his own needs and that bedrooms and bedtimes might be a new experience for him.

Modeling the story after The Jungle Book and the Curious George stories, Bill and Karen described the life of an orphaned chimp, growing up in the wild jungle. In the jungle, he was free to do what ever he wanted whenever he wanted. Sometimes the chimp loved the freedom of the jungle. But when food was scarce and he could not find a dry place to sleep during the rainy season, the chimp longed for a home like the other monkeys had. Bill and Karen continued to tell Robert about the mishaps and fun the chimp had on his own in the jungle. The day's story ended with the chimp staring straight into the eyes of a strange creature that walked on two legs all the time. As usual, Robert feigned disinterest when the story was over but asked when he would get to hear the end. Later that day, Bill and Karen completed the narrative. The kind man who found him in the jungle named the chimp Charlie. Charlie didn't know his name and didn't always come when the man called. He didn't misbehave on purpose; he just did not know. Life in the jungle was very different from life in the city. Sometimes the chimp missed his freedom and was angry with the man. He did not like rules. But the man was kind and very patient. He taught Charlie all about hot dogs and other strange and yummy foods, about swinging on the tire swing instead of telephone wires, and about soft beds that were never cold and wet. They emphasized that Charlie was not a bad chimp; he just had a lot to learn.

Problem-solving tips

Understanding the meaning of the child's behavior is the key to successful child narratives. If the meaning is not addressed, the behavior may not change. For example, lying is a common and frustrating problem. The reason for the lying may be very different and is dependent on the child's inner working model. A narrative to address the problem of lying might be about a little girl who believes everything she wishes is true, which addresses a developmental need. It may also be about a tiger that changes his stripes and his story to keep anyone from knowing the deep, dark ugliness he hides inside. The second narrative would attempt to shift the child's negative conclusions related to the events of the past. Some commonly asked questions are answered below.

My child seems to enjoy the stories. He even asks for them, but I'm not sure they are changing his behavior

Be sure the task is developmentally appropriate and within the child's capabilities. If there are developmental prerequisites necessary to achieve the desired behavior change, a series of developmental narratives may be needed to help the child catch up. The problem behaviors exhibited by the child may have developed while he lived in a chaotic, abusive situation. A behavior, like hoarding food, helped him survive. Giving up that behavior is a risk. It may require a level of trust in the adults around him of which the child is not yet capable. Address the underlying anxiety about change in future narratives. Give the child permission to stay stuck as long as he needs to. Reassure him that he is loved and supported as he experiments with new behaviors.

I'm afraid I'm telling too many stories. Will my child get overloaded?

Many children look forward to a daily story time and will even remind parents when the routine is altered. Some parents have developed a cast of characters that they can use to vary the stories and prevent boredom. Telling silly, adventurous stories with the child's favorite character that have no particular moral message or teaching content should prevent boredom and resistance.

I'm not very creative. Where can I get ideas for stories?

The only requirement for Family Attachment Narrative Therapy is love and a firm commitment to the child. Mother's (or father's) intuition, empathy, and attunement are the keys to discovering the child's underlying feelings and the meaning of her behavior. Once the meaning is unlocked, the exact words of the narrative matter less. The ritual of cuddling together, talking, listening, and demonstrating that the child is understood may facilitate change even if the story is not award-winning material. There are many children's books that teach values and moral behavior. Flipping through a few at the local library may get the creative juices flowing. Family, friends, and other parents may be able to help construct narratives as well.

Summary

Children who did not experience the attuned responses of a loving parent in the early years of life may have difficulty in future relationships. A negative inner working model gives rise to problem behaviors. Children who have been traumatized or who have delays in adaptive functioning present foster and adoptive parents with challenges that beat every parenting technique they can think of. Parents use successful child narratives with children to teach and model new behavior. The key to changing a child's behavior is not gaining control over the child. It is not finding a reinforcement or consequence that will work better. The key is discovering the child's inner working model and the meaning of the behavior. Then when she is ready to make a new choice, stories allow the child to see other behavior options.

Conclusion

Once there were two women, who never knew each other.
One you do not remember, the other you call Mother.

Life is about connections: connections between people, between people and their community, between communities and the world. We believe that humans are designed to be in relationship with others. We also believe that early life interactions are especially critical, because they form the foundation for an internal model of the self and of relationships with other people. Whether positive or negative, that model guides and directs behavior. The importance of a healthy attachment or connection between an infant and caregiver cannot be overstated. It is the basis for the model and for the child's future relationships and behavior in society. Secure attachment happens when the parents and children spend time together. It is a process. Kids need both quantity and quality time. Sensitive, attuned care facilitates a healthy sense of self and a healthy internal model of what relationships can be. A secure attachment is vital to the growth of the children.

When first relationships do not provide the kind of emotional and physical care that is required for healthy growth and development, the individual may face multiple challenges throughout his life span. Fortunately, recognition of the importance of early attachment relationships is gaining increased acceptance, and strategies are being developed to ameliorate the effects of less than optimal early life interactions. Still, there are far too many children that suffer maltreatment and inadequate parental care when young. This sad fact is evidenced by the increasing case loads of social workers in social service departments around the world. Change must occur in families and in our society as a whole to prevent the disaster of wounded children. We need to fully support the parents and families that welcome these children into their homes. This support needs to be in terms of adequate financial, educational, and other resources – regardless of the legal status of the relationship. The loving home of a family offers the best hope for correcting the damage from inadequate early life attachment relationships. The bond between parent and child must be recognized and nurtured by our society.

About resources

It is not lack of effort or knowledge that leads parents to us, but rather a realization that techniques to merely manage behavior with their child are not enough. Narratives work to bond, heal, and teach. The individualized stories address the underlying mistaken beliefs and the negative inner working model that drives challenging behaviors. Daily story times build bonds between parents and children. Sensitive redoing of early life narratives helps children resolve traumatic experiences and losses. Captivating characters model new behaviors that the child can choose to use when ready. However, telling stories while the child is pounding his sister's head into the wall does not seem practical or wise. At the moment parents must act swiftly to protect their children. Later, after tempers have cooled, a story about jealousy and rivalry may help resolve the underlying feelings of insecurity. Over the years, we have encountered some parenting resources that contribute to the attachment process and others that seem counter to connecting with kids. Avoid parenting techniques that emphasize controlling the child or rely only on consequences to shape and teach behavior. Instead, search out tools that nurture the child, help the child increase self-awareness and her ability to regulate emotions, and experience success.

A wide range of parenting techniques and strategies may all be useful at various times with a particular child. No one parenting methodology is going to work all the time, with all kids. The following resources contain nurturing approaches that focus on the strengths of the child.

- *Parenting the Hurt Child: Helping Adoptive Families Heal and Grow,* by Greg Keck and Regina Kupecky. Colorado Springs, Colorado: Piñon Press, 2002.

- *For All Things A Season: An Essential Guide to a Peaceful Parent/Child Relationship,* by B. Bryan Post. Oklahoma: M. Brynn Publishing, 2003.

- *Transforming the Difficult Child: The Nurtured Heart Approach,* by Howard Glasser and Jennifer Easley. Tucson, Arizona: Center for the Difficult Child, 1999.

- *Attaching in Adoption: Practical Tools for Today's Parents*, by Deborah D. Gray. Indianapolis, Indiana: Perspectives Press, 2002.

A companion manual to this book, *Parenting with Stories: Creating a Foundation of Attachment for Parenting Your Child*, by Melissa Nichols, Denise B. Lacher, and Joanne C. May (Deephaven, Minnesota: Family Attachment and Counseling Center, 2002), is designed as a workbook to help parents create stories for their child. This manual is useful by itself, or in workshops that teach the technique of creating stories.

A final word

We hope this book has been useful for parents who are searching for a way to connect or reconnect with a troubled child. We want to emphasize once again that we believe parents are in the best position to reach and to help their children. But occasionally parents do need additional help from professionals. The tremendous stresses of rearing a child with a history of trauma and disruptions in attachment relationships may have temporarily frustrated their capacity for attunement. Parents should seek professionals that listen and honor the knowledge they have about their child. The role of the parent must be supported, even elevated, in order to reactivate their attunement capacity. Professionals that take on the role of guru may undercut the parents and render them powerless to help their child resolve attachment issues. We believe that parents should be included in the therapy process as the primary healing agent. Parents have an innate ability to understand and respond to their child's cues. Looking beyond the behavior to discover the child's inner working model may not come naturally at first. However, focusing on the why of behavior effectively changes day-to-day parenting and leads to construction of narratives that can shift the inner working model. Intimate knowledge of the child's thoughts and feelings permits parents to construct a unique, one of a kind narrative. Instead of a "one size fits all" story, parents insert their own idiosyncrasies into every creation. It's a bestseller for an audience of one.

EMDR

Trauma narratives told by parents may provide a coherent life story for the child. During the telling, the events may become desensitized. The parents' presence and availability provide a secure base so that the child does not become dysregulated during the story. Eventually, the child becomes bored with it. Parents may see a reduction in anxiety and behaviors related to the trauma. Narratives also seem to shift the negative meaning the child attributed to the event and to himself. A child who believed that he was bad and deserving of abuse and abandonment may begin to accept the possibility that, like all babies, he deserved attention and love. He may question the conclusion that what happened was his fault. In some cases the extent and severity of the trauma may be beyond that which parents feel comfortable handling in a narrative.

Seeking out professionals trained in Eye Movement Desensitization and Reprocessing (EMDR) to assist in helping the child heal from past abuse, neglect, and losses may be advisable. Eye Movement Desensitization and Reprocessing was discovered and developed by Francine Shapiro in 1987. It is postulated that EMDR provides a mechanism for healing on neurological, physiological, emotional, and cognitive levels. Shapiro (1995) asserts that trauma obstructs a natural information processing system. The event remains in memory in its anxiety-producing form. Images, strong feelings, and physical sensations are then triggered by a multitude of stimuli encountered in everyday life. The bilateral stimulation of EMDR (eye movement, hand taps, auditory or tactile stimuli) seems to reactivate the information processing system. Unobstructed, the memory is now processed and loses its emotional and physical impact. The child is enabled to consider new conclusions about the event. For more information on EMDR visit the website: www.EMDR.com.

Story Construction Guide

- What would you like to work on with your child?

- What is the message you would like the story to convey?

- What perspective (first or third person) seems most appropriate for your situation and message?

- In the first person perspective, you may use your own experience or story that your child may identify with to communicate the message to your child. Describe the events of the experience...

- Think about the emotional content: how can you convey the emotions both verbally and nonverbally?

- If you are considering using the third person perspective, with what character might your child identify?
  - Describe the appearance of the character...

  - Describe the setting in which the story takes place...

- Referring back to the message you would like to convey, what plot would capture your child's interest while communicating the message?

- What are the character's thoughts, feelings, and actions as the plot unfolds?

- Would any story aides be helpful? If so, what?

References

Achenbach, T.M. and Rescorla, L.A. (2001) *Manual for the ASEBA School-Age Forms and Profiles.* Burlington, VT: Universtiy of Vermont Research Center for Children, Youth and Families.

Ainsworth, M.D.S. (1967) *Infancy in Uganda: Infant Care and the Growth of Attachment.* Baltimore, MD: Johns Hopkins Press.

Ainsworth, M.D.S., Blehar, M., Waters, E., and Wall, S. (1978) *Patterns of Attachment.* Hillsdale, NJ: Erlbaum.

Belsky, J. and Cassidy, J. (1994) "Attachment: theory and evidence." In M.L. Rutter, D.F. Hay, and S. Baron-Cohen (eds) *Development Through Life: A Handbook for Clinicians.* Oxford: Blackwell.

Bowlby, J. (1969/1982) *Attachment and Loss, Vol. 1. Attachment.* New York: Basic Books.

Bowlby, J. (1973) *Attachment and Loss, Vol. 2. Separation.* New York: Basic Books.

Bowlby, J. (1980) *Attachment and Loss, Vol. 3. Loss.* New York: Basic Books.

Bowlby, J. (1988) *A Secure Base.* New York: Basic Books.

Bretherton, I. (1985) "Attachment theory: retrospect and prospect." In I. Bretherton and E. Waters (eds) *Growing Points of Attachment Theory and Research, Monographs of the Society for Research in Child Development 50* (1–2, Serial No. 209).

Bretherton, I. (1987) "New perspectives on attachment relations: security, communication, and internal working models." In J. Osofsky (ed) *Handbook of Infant Development.* New York: Wiley.

Bretherton, I. and Munholland, K.A. (1999) "Internal working models in attachment relationships: a construct revisited." In J. Cassidy and P.R. Shaver (eds) *Handbook of Attachment: Theory, Research and Clinical Applications.* New York: Guilford Press.

Bruner, J. (1987) "Life as narrative." *Social Research 4*, 1, 11–32.

Caplan, F. (1973) *The First Twelve Months of Life: Your Baby's Growth Month by Month.* New York: Perigree Putnam.

Carlson, E.A. and Sroufe, L.A. (1995) "Contributions of attachment theory to developmental psychopathology." In D. Cicchetti and C.J. Cohen (eds) *Developmental Psychopathology* (Vol. 1). New York: Wiley.

Chesney, M. and Spencer, M.J. (2004) *Easing the Transition from Institutional to Family Life.* Minneapolis, MN: International Adoption Clinic, University of Minnesota. www.peds.umn.edu/iac/downloads/index.html, downloaded July 14 2004

Collin, P.H. (ed) (1999) *Webster's Student Dictionary.* New York: Barnes and Noble.

Cozolino, L.J. (2002) *The Neuroscience of Psychotherapy: Building and Rebuilding the Human Brain.* New York: W.W. Norton.

Dreikurs, R. with Soltz, V. (1990) *Children: The Challenge.* New York: Plume Penguin.

Egeland, B., Yates, T., Appleyard, K., and van Dulmen, M. (2002) "The long-term consequences of maltreatment in the early years: a developmental pathway model to antisocial behavior." *Children's Services: Social Policy, Research, and Practice 5,* 4, 249–260.

Elicker, J., Egeland, M., and Sroufe, L.A. (1992) "Predicting peer competence and peer relationships from early parent–child relationships." In R.D. Parke and G.W. Ladd (eds) *Family–Peer Relationships: Modes of Linkage.* Hillsdale, NJ: Erlbaum.

Erickson, M.F., Sroufe, L.A., and Egeland, B. (1985) "The relationship between quality of attachment and behavior problems in preschool in a high-risk sample." In I. Bretherton and E. Waters (eds) Growing Points of Attachment Theory and Research, *Monographs of the Society for Research in Child Development 50* (1–2, Serial No. 209).

Gurganus, S. (2002) *A Reliability and Validity Study of the May-Nichols Child Behavior Rating Scale.* Unpublished doctoral dissertation, Minnesota School of Professional Psychology.

Jacobvitz, D. and Hazen, N. (1999) "Developmental pathways from infant disorganization to childhood peer relationships." In J. Solomon and C. George (eds) *Attachment Disorganization.* New York: Guilford Press.

Jernberg, A.M. and Booth, P.B. (1999) *Theraplay: Helping Parents and Children Build Better Relationships through Attachment Based Play,* 2nd edn. San Francisco: Jossey-Bass Publishers.

Johnson, D. (2004) *The Short- and Long-Term Effects of Early Childhood Deprivation on Health and Development.* Minneapolis, MN: International Adoption Clinic, University of Minnesota. www.peds.umn.edu/iac/downloads/index.html, downloaded July 14 2004

Keck, G.C. and Kupecky, R.M. (1995) *Adopting the Hurt Child.* Colorado Springs, CO: Piñon Press.

Liotti, G. (1999) "Disorganization of attachment as a model for understanding dissociative psychopathology." In J. Solomon and C. George (eds) *Attachment Disorganization.* New York: Guilford Press.

Lyons-Ruth, K. (1996) "Attachment relationships among children with aggressive behavior problems: the role of disorganized early attachment patterns." *Journal of Consulting and Clinical Psychology 64,* 1, 64–73.

Lyons-Ruth, K. and Jacobvitz, D. (1999) "Attachment disorganization: unresolved loss, relational violence, and lapses in behavioral and attentional strategies." In J. Cassidy and P.R. Shaver (eds) *Handbook of Attachment: Theory, Research and Clinical Applications.* New York: Guilford Press.

Main, M. and Cassidy, J. (1988) "Categories of response to reunion with the parent at age 6: predictable from infant attachment classifications and stable over a 1-month period." *Developmental Psychology 24,* 3, 415–426.

Main, M. and Solomon, J. (1986) "Discovery of a new, insecure-disorganized/disoriented attachment pattern." In T.B. Brazelton and M. Youngman (eds) *Affective Development in Infancy* Norwood, NJ: Ablex.

Main, M. and Solomon, J. (1990) "Procedures for identifying infants as disorganized/disoriented during the Ainsworth Strange Situation." In M.T. Greenberg, D. Cicchetti, and E.M. Cummings (eds) *Attachment in the Preschool Years.* Chicago, IL: University of Chicago Press.

Main, M., Kaplan, N., and Cassidy, J. (1985) "Security in infancy, childhood, and adulthood: A move to the next level of representation." In I. Bretherton and E. Waters (eds) Growing Points of Attachment Theory and Research, *Monographs of the Society for Research in Child Development 50* (1–2, Serial No. 209).

May, J.C. and Nichols, T. (1997) *Child Behavior Rating Scale.* Deephaven, MN: Family Attachment and Counseling Center.

Perry, B. (1997) "Incubated in terror: neurodevelopmental factors in the cycle of violence." In J. Osofsky (ed) *Children in a Violent Society.* New York: Guilford Press.

Perry, B., Pollard, R., Blakely, T., Baker, W., and Vigilante, D. (1995) "Childhood trauma, the neurobiology of adaptation, and use-dependent development of the brain: how states become traits." *Infant Mental Health Journal 16,* 271–291.

Piaget, J. and Inhelder, B. (1969) *The Psychology of the Child.* New York: Basic Books.

Schoenfield, P. (undated) *Paul Schoenfield Four Parables, Vaudeville, Klezmer Rondos Compact Disc liner notes.* Argo 440 212–2 (1994).

Schore, A.N. (1994) *Affect Regulation and the Origin of the Self: The Neurobiology of Emotional Development.* Hillsdale, NJ: Erlbaum.

Schore, A.N. (1998) "Early shame experiences and brain development." In P. Gilbert and B. Andrews (eds) *Shame: Interpersonal Behavior, Psychopathology and Culture.* New York: Oxford University Press.

Schore, A.N. (2001a) "Effects of a secure attachment relationship on right brain development, affect regulation, and infant mental health." *Infant Mental Health Journal 22,* 1–2, 7–66.

Schore, A.N. (2001b) "The effects of early relational trauma on right brain development, affect regulation, and infant mental health." *Infant Mental Health Journal 22,* 1–2, 201–269.

Shapiro, F. (1995) *Eye Movement Desensitization and Reprocessing: Basic Principles, Protocols, and Procedures.* New York: Guilford Press.

Siegel, D.J. (1999) *The Developing Mind: How Relationships and the Brain Interact to Shape Who We Are.* New York: Guilford Press.

Siegel, D.J. (2001) "Toward an interpersonal neurobiology of the developing mind: attachment relationships, 'mindsight,' and neural integration." *Infant Mental Health Journal 22,* 1–2, 7–66.

Siegel, D.J. and Hartzell, M. (2003) *Parenting from the Inside Out: How a Deeper Self-understanding Can Help You Raise Children Who Thrive.* New York: Tarcher Putnam.

Sparrow, S.S., Balla, D.A., and Cicchetti, D.V. (1984) *Interview Edition Survey Form Manual Vineland Adaptive Behavior Scales.* Circle Pines, MN: American Guidance Service.

Spock, B. (1945) *The Common Sense Book of Baby and Child Care.* New York: Duell, Sloan, and Pearce.

Sroufe, L.A. (1996) *Emotional Development: The Organization of Emotional Life in the Early Years.* New York: Cambridge University Press.

Stern, D.N. (1985) *The Interpersonal World of the Infant.* New York: W.H. Freeman.

van der Kolk, B.A. (1996) "The complexity of adaptation to trauma: self-regulation, stimulus discrimination, and characterological development." In B.A. van der Kolk, A.C. McFarlane, and L. Weisaeth (eds) *Traumatic Stress: The Effects of Overwhelming Experience on Mind, Body, and Society.* New York: Guilford.

van der Kolk, B.A. and Fisler, R.E. (1994) "Childhood abuse and neglect and loss of self-regulation." *Bulletin of the Menninger Clinic 58*, 2, 145–168.

White, B.L. (1975) *The First Three Years of Life.* New York: Avon Books.

Subject Index

Author Index